Social implications in the philosophy of Vivekananda

MANGALYA B.

CONTENTS

                                                                                                     Pages

PREFACE

CHAPTER I   **INTRODUCTION**   **1-29**

- The relevance of social philosophy
- Concept of Society
- Social Structure of Ancient, Medieval and Modern Periods
- Evolution of Indian Social Thought-From Ancient to the Modern Period
- Objectives of the Study
- Review of Literature
- Methodology
- Significance of the Study
- Lay out of the Thesis

CHAPTER II   **SOCIO-CULTURAL BACKGROUND OF THE PHILOSOPHY OF VIVEKANANDA**   **30-72**

- Social Milieu of Vivekananda's Thought
- Parental Influences
- The Impact of Education
- The Influence of Sri Ramakrishna and His Teachings
- Cultural Background of Vivekananda's Thought
- Renaissance Period and its Impact
- Intellectual Background of Vivekananda's Philosophy
- Influence of Vedanta thought
- Bhagavat Gita and its Influence
- Influence of Buddhistic Ideas
- Influence of the Teachings of Jesus Christ

CHAPTER III   THE METAPHYSICAL PERSPECTIVES OF VIVEKANANDA   73-108

- Reconciliation of Advaita, Visistadvaita and Dvaita Thoughts
- Concept of Brahman
- Concept of World
- Concept of Maya
- Concept of Man
- Four Yogas of Liberation
- Raja-Yoga
- Karma-Yoga
- Bhakti-Yoga
- Jnana-Yoga

CHAPTER IV   THE SOCIAL IDEAS OF VIVEKANANDA   109-167

- Neo-Vedanta Thought- Synthesis of Theory and Practice
- Concept of Universal Religion- Harnessing of Different Paths
- Thoughts on Eastern Spiritualism and Western Materialism
- Individualistic Approach of the West and Socialistic Approach of the East
- Synthesis of Tradition and Modernity
- Concept of Society- 'the One and the Many'
- Diversity as an Essential Aspect of Society
- Advocate of Caste Mobility
- Privilege as a bane to society
- Equality of Opportunity
- Cultural Upheaval of the Masses
- Democratization of Education
- Demerits of Indian Educational System

- Man-making Education
- Women as the main component of Society
- Advocate of Gender Equality
- Views Regarding the Institution of Marriage
- Role of Youth in Social Service

CHAPTER 5   CONCLUSION   **168-198**

BIBLIOGRAPHY   **199-207**

CHAPTER-1

INTRODUCTION

The legacy of Swami Vivekananda is perennial for he is a great social reformer, religious teacher and a patriot saint but above all an unparallel visionary. It is in this context that the question that who can be regarded as a philosopher comes to one's mind. There is no doubt on the fact that his ideas and messages concerning different aspects of religion, youth, education, faith, character-building as well as social ideals remain most inspiring and rejuvenating to his readers all over the world. For these reasons, one cannot regard him as merely a dull dispenser of thought, but as a man who has heart to feel, head to think, hand to work and who feels in his inner-self the spiritual unity of all existence. These are the qualities which are not exclusively attributed to a reformer or a saint, but to a philosopher also.

A true philosophy must be rational, critical and exposing the contents of theology, social and political sciences and also the right instrument and foundation of all action and duty and must assist one to achieve intellectual balance and behavioural competence.[1] Accordingly it is no mere agglomeration of certain views and conceptions of the outside world. And a philosopher is not a man who loses himself in quests unconnected with life's problems, nor can he concern himself with externals only, forgetting the significance of the inner life. A balance and an attempt at

---

[1] K. Satchidananda Murthy, *Philosophy of India: Tradition, Teaching and Research,* (New Delhi: Motilal Banarsidass in association with ICPR, 1985), p.VII.

harmony between these is what an authentic philosophy recommends. Philosophy cannot be limited only to abstract ideas. It includes those ideas but it also includes other ideas. It concerns the whole of man, and not only his abstract thoughts, intellect, feelings, body or relation to the world around him. A philosopher like any other human being has to play a role in the society. The function of a philosopher is not just to give a theory which has no relevance to social context, but to critically reflect over them and find ways of understanding the changing situations. Philosophy and life are closely tied together. The essence of philosophy for an individual includes of necessity, the why and wherefore of his own existence. It will consciously or subconsciously form the basis on which he leads his life.[2] There are philosophical questions and problems in all areas of human enquiry and practice. Hence it is said that the whole world seems to be the subject matter of philosophical enquiry and every person has practised the art of thinking in some form or other. It develops a comprehensive system of thought about the universe and the life as a whole. Philosophical problems can be categorized into three such as those related to knowledge and experience, those related to supreme Good and Existence and those related to Values. It is not through sentimentality and emotional approaches that one can understand life. A person who says that whatever the society gives is the right course of action, cannot be called a philosopher. And a thought which speaks merely of the highest Reality without reference to everyday life will not be of much use to

---

[2] P.J. Saher, *Eastern Wisdom and Western Thought* (London: Allen and Unwin, 1969), p.207.

humankind. Hence the study of philosophy must be concerned with the nature of human society.

Conceptual thought is needed for solving and clarifying the basic normative questions which cannot be answered by empirical investigation and philosophy mainly aim at the conceptual aspects of understanding in any field of study. Philosophizing is certainly not identical with socialization, but we cannot think of philosophical problems without empirical data. But the conceptual thinking and its practice cannot be placed in a sharp dichotomy. Theory and action, like thought and action always influence each other. Dating back to Socrates and Marx it has been argued that pure philosophical theory without practical application was untenable. Practical utility may not be the goal of all the philosophical endeavours, It may be the natural consequence of endeavours. When the efforts are aimed at practical results in the pursuit of a philosophical theory, one will fail to reach his goal. It is when one pursues knowledge in a dispassionate way, unfettered by any external considerations; he will reach a theory, from which practical advantage flow naturally. The state is somewhat similar to the paradox of hedonism in which a person never attains happiness so long as he aims at it. Perhaps, this may be the reason why the classical philosophers have set before themselves the goal of attaining knowledge of ultimate Reality only through a method unrestricted by pragmatic considerations. But it may also be relevant to state that it is not easy to define a philosophical theory which is merely theoretical in character. Its practical application may remain hidden, implicit and unnoticed. This was what happened in the thoughts of Hegel and Sankara.[3] Their abstract philosophical theory of Absolute Idealism is not as barren as it appeared. Its basic tenet of the ultimate Reality being one universal spirit pervading all things definitely has its social implication. But so long as the practical application is kept under wraps and its abstractness is attenuated, it can never effect change in a social group or a community which consist of not only elites and intellectuals but also average and ordinary men. If it exposes its workability and concreteness it may be appealing to the common man and thereby perceptible in the social life of the people. Hence it stands for an understanding and a method of solving the diverse problems of life and existence. No brief definition expresses the richness and variety of philosophy. Philosophy cannot be placed under a particular area as it is *weltanschauung*, it must be universal in its scope. Therefore it embraces ideas which originate not only in any particular country in a particular form but in all countries and in all periods of civilization. Not all ideas are philosophical, but only those which are true, useful, in harmony with the world idea, and able to survive the test of practice and applicability.[4] Neither can it be categorized as purely speculative nor can it be treated as purely practical. It is quite unlike any other field because of its uniqueness both in its method and breadth of its subject matter. Thought and reality, facts and values are inseparable. Being so Philosophy is not only normative, postulating ideals of what is socially desirable and necessary, but has to remain a

---

[3] Dharmendra Goel, *Philosophy And Social Change* (Delhi: Ajanta Publications,1989), p.245.
[4] Paul Brunton, *Perspectives* (New York: Larson Publications, 1984), p.251.

critique of different ideals and has to temper the anomalies and reconcile them using reason and, thereafter, interlacing these with most effective steps and administer method for their actualization.[5] Thus the definition of philosophy itself will suggest whether philosophy is socially relevant or not.

The Relevance of Social Philosophy

The social philosophy analyses many facets of social life of man in a philosophical background. It emanates from a deep concern for man and his social existence and delves deep into the relationship between the individual and his society and tries to harmonize personal life with social life. Though social philosophy is believed to be a new branch of study, the idea of social philosophy had been there in early period of human civilization. It aims at an all round development of society by addressing various social issues that stand in the way of its progress, thereby creating favourable condition for life. Social philosophy of any age reflects the agonies and sufferings of the age and suggests a way out of them by stressing the ideals of individual and social happiness.[6] It is therefore creative and critical in its approach. The philosophy is much needed for implementing a change in a social system when the beliefs and ideas prevailing earlier do not tally anymore with the public affairs and perceived requirements do not function in a harmonious way. Whenever a social change happens as the result of disturbance of the harmony of the system and if the

---

[5] Dharmendra Goel, *op.cit.*, p.4.

[6] Aniruddha Jha, *Social Philosophy of Bertrand Russell* (Delhi: Ajanta Publications,1978), p.2.

existing beliefs and thoughts do not fit in the new social set up, it is the philosopher's function to anticipate a future society by reflecting over the existing rules, principles and conventions in order to lessen the friction, thus paving the way for social cohesion and betterment.

Social philosophy also contains the thought that stresses the reflective assessments and critique of society and culture in the light of supreme good of man. Values, ethical theories and the messy facts of human social arrangements are discussed in it. For most of the Western philosophers the validity of social values is assessed by a moral criterion. But Indian thinkers have taken both spiritual and moral values into consideration.[7] The social philosophy as the philosophy of values assesses social relations and the authenticity of the prevailing social methods in the light of the supreme ideal. It is for this reason that J.S. Mackenzie holds it as "an effort to study values, ends, ideals, not primarily what exists or has existed or may be expected to exist, but rather the meaning and worth of these modes of existence."[8]

Thus social philosophy examines and interprets the facts and ideals of human life and thereby exposes the institutions and principles that govern the society. A person who says that whatever the society gives is the right course of action, cannot be called a social philosopher. A philosopher as a creative thinker cannot be thought of a mere automation, he is not a person who says whatever the society gives is the right course of action instead he detaches himself from his social set-up by critically

---

[7] Dr. Ramnath Sharma, *Social Philosophy* (Meerut: Kedar Nath Ram Nath, n.d.), p.3.
[8] J.S.Mackenzie, *Outlines of Social Philosophy* (London: George Allen and Unwin Ltd., 1952), p.14.

examining and reflecting over even his own created values. Robert N. Beck defined social philosophy as a "philosophic critique of social process with reference to the principles underlying social structure and functions."[9] It is an examination and analysis of facts and ideals of human life and thereby exposes the institutions and principles which govern the society. Its roots lie in a perceived divergence between how a society has been functioning leading it to crises and chaos and how it should function with a view for realizing the ideals of a happy life. Vivekananda, as a social thinker also tried to do the same within the Indian context analyzing its short comings and tried to rectify it with ideals in the Vedanta philosophy and the Western ideals of society and left his indelible mark on Indian thinking.

Concept of Society

The term society has its derivation from the Latin word 'societas' which means 'to share' or 'to unite'. Man lived in society from the very beginning. As social life is instinctive with men, they are tied in mutual relations which they cannot afford to exist one without the other. Necessity also compels him to lead a social life. Man needs the context of other human beings for his very humanization. Thus a man who is incapable of sharing a pattern of life is either above or below humanity. This is what the renowned Aristotlean dictum says while pointing out the solitary or the self-sufficient man as either a God or a beast.[10] Though societies were first formed for

---

[9] Robert. N. Beck, *Hand Book of Social Philosophy* cited in P. George Victor, *Social Philosophy of Vedanta* (NewDelhi: K.P. Bagchi and Company,1991), p.2.
[10] Jonathan Lear, *Aristotle: the Desire to Understand* (United Kingdom: Cambridge University Press, 1999), p.101.

the sake of life, later they were maintained for the purpose of leading a good life.[11] People incapable of feeling remorse are labeled as antisocial. Viewed from this perspective social living represent the acme of human culture and civilization. An individual is a means for social interaction. He is not only himself, but is in solidarity with all of his kind.

Society is not something alien imposed on man. There is a profound integration of the social destiny with that of the individual. Dr.S.Radhakrishnan views human society as an attempt to express in social life the cosmic purpose which has other ways of expression in the material and the spiritual planes.[12] Being a member of society everyone is aware of the social activity and is affected by the activities of other members of society. Each person has his own unique outlook towards society and they are also more or less aware of the ideologies prevalent in the society. Both similarity and dissimilarity are to be found in society. Unity in diversity forms the basic trait of social relations. This diversity and dissimilarity breeds interdependence among the social units and causes division of labour which leads to mutual cooperation and organization. Such social interconnection and interaction can have an ethical dimension also. In the animal world there is no organization or system which may be called societies. Hence a mere aggregate of individuals does not constitute a society as a mere accumulation of bricks does not constitute a building. Societies exist only in the interactions of persons, but all our behavior is rule

---

[11] J.S.Mackenzie, *op.cit.*, p.35.
[12] S.Radhakrishnan, *Eastern Religions and Western Thought* (London: Allen and Unwin, 1989), p.355.

governed and rules necessarily have universality. We can never think of a society which does not have common standards and rules. Social laws and societies are products of cultural orientation. The real problem in society is that of ensuring a harmonious living, balancing of an individual's inner and outer life, adjustment of the relationship between individuals and groups of people and thereby making the society improve constantly.[13] The perfection that may not be achieved individually may be attained by working collectively as a group, counteracting, equipoising, adjusting and fulfilling one another.[14] This would lead to harmony by a number of persons and would make solution to every pressing problem like religious intolerance, cultural exclusiveness and blind fanaticism. A harmony of love and wisdom is the key required for a better society.

Social Structure in Ancient, Medieval and Modern India

The Indian social philosophy in different ages has its own thought which reveals the hidden relation between the individual and society. Its beginning can be traced from ancient scriptures of *Srutis* and *Smritis*. They emerge as the result of the reflective thinking of the ancient Indian seers for the purpose of providing a qualitative and healthy social life. Though the unique feature of Indian social philosophy is its emphasis on spirituality and spiritual development of the individual, it does not turn its face towards material advancements. This is evident in its idea of

---

[13] Jawaharlal Nehru, *Discovery of India* (Calcutta: Oxford University Press, 1999), p.31.
[14] SwamiVivekananda, *The Complete Works of SwamiVivekananda* (Kolkata: Advaita Ashrama, 2003), Vol.4, p. 336.

purusharthas, the principle value system in India which regards *dharma, artha, kama* and *moksha*[15] as the four values that a man has to seek in his life. Of these, *Dharma* implies the laws or principle, on which the society is based, *artha* indicates wealth, *Kama* as the desire in every person and *moksha* stands for liberation. Among these four pursuits, the middle two are materialistic values. They nevertheless have their place in the overall scheme of life. Some level of material prosperity and the enjoyment of ordinary pleasure of life by at least a part of the population are necessary for society to flourish and continue. *Artha* and *kama* are to be gained on the basis of *dharma* with the aim of attaining *moksha*. *Dharma* and *moksha* are the means and goals of spiritual culture and are necessary for the proper functioning of the social order. The ultimate end of life, *moksha* entails concentration of all human energies inward in the world of spirit which paves the way for a synthetic vision of unity of the One and many. The triple ends of *dharma, artha* and *kama* are the social manifestations of the three aspects of human consciousness namely thought, action and desire. If there is unwarranted suppression of any of these basic urges of man, the result will be restlessness in the individual and conflict in the society. Hence Indian ethics upholds an integral approach with regard to the aim of life. There are many instances in history of the balance between the society and the individual being lost due to the excessive emphasis laid upon single aspect of life. Buddhists, Christians, among them St.Paul and Tartulian and priests of middle ages in Europe laid excessive emphasis on abstention with the result of which there arose a strong reaction in the

---

[15] S.Radhakrishnan, *op.cit.*, p.351.

direction of morality.[16] Indian seers, perhaps, were acquainted with these psychological possibilities. They thus embraced an integral approach which ensures a stable and balanced base for the individual and the organization of society.

Another distinguishing feature the ancient Indian society had was the arrangement of its social structure in accordance with the system of *Ashrama* and *Varna*. The scheme unifies the interest of the individual and the group. There need not be any conflict between the individual and the group life as both are mutually interdependent. The purpose of the system is to put the different powers of man to proper and productive uses in order to maintain a balanced state of society. Thus a harmonious social order was formed with the system of *Varnasramadharma* which coalesces the four stages of man's life and four different types of personalities forming the four divisions of society. *Ashramas*, the step in the journey of life is meant for the ordering of man in different stages of life.[17] During *Bramacharya ashrama* one is supposed to devote time in acquiring education by keeping away from passions and desire. This makes him possible to lead a better individual life and prepares the background for useful absorption in social life. After the completion of education one has to enter into *Grihastashrama* leading a family life. Here a man is required to give birth to children and enrich his family in the spirit of responsible

---

[16] Dr.Vatsyayan, *History of Social Thought* (Meerut: Kedarnath Ramnath, n.d.), pp.178-9.
[17] Robert.A,McDermott, ed., *The Basic Writings of S. Radhakrishnan* (Mumbai: Jaico Publishing House,2007), p.212.

parenthood.[18] Meanwhile he has to work for the welfare of the society. After the fulfillment of family duties he has to lead a life of solitude and to practise yoga. Here though he lives in the world, he does not participate in any of the social activities except as a guide or advisor of the young. This stage of *vanaprastha* is succeeded by *sannyasa*, a life of renunciation which is concerned with the spiritual fulfillment of the individual himself. Such a man becomes the benefactor of the whole living world. Thus these stages of life were meant not to suppress the desires in man but to sublimate them. The man's life were channelized in the right direction and utilized properly through the exercise of the *ashrama* system.

Indian social system introduced some sort of perfection into the social order by bringing together man of different capacities and different tastes into an ordered system. The word '*varna*' comes from the root '*vri*' giving the meaning of choice. In this way, *varna* is that which a person chooses according to his nature and his work. Hence Varna system in ancient period does not claim for any privileges. On the other hand it was meant for a division of labour[19] and for an orderly progress of work in society. The system is based on four different tendencies common in man- *satvika, sathvika-rajasika, rajasika-tamasika* and *tamasika*. The *satvika* stands for the teacher-class, *sathvika-rajasika* for administration class, *rajasika-tamasika* for business class and the last one stands for the class of workers. Society has many kinds of

---

[18] Dr. Nirmala Tandon, *Contemporary Indian Ethics* (Mumbai: English Edition Publishers and Distributors (India) Pvt. Ltd., n.d.), p.4.
[19] M.B. Chande, *Indian Philosophy in Modern Times* (NewDelhi: Atlantic Publishers and Distributors, 2000), p.42.

requirements – it needs the service of workers (*Sudras*), economic class (*Vaisyas*), administrators (*Kshatriyas*) as well as thinkers (*Brahmins*).

This system of social stratification that prevailed in Indian society was first traced in the *purusa-sukta* of RigVeda. In it society is equated with Cosmic *Purusa* or organic union with its many different components and all are essentially complete while preserving the diversity. It shows that the society functions as a well co ordinate single unit; in it none is inferior to the other. All are equally important and cooperative action of all these components are essential for the proper functioning of society. Originally, this division into different *Varnas* is the stepping stone to civilization. By fulfilling the demands of both the inner and the outer life of the individual, it aimed at social progress. But the scheme later deteriorated into an obnoxious one because of the claim of superiority and privileges by certain sections of the society on the basis of birth.

Varna system exercised in ancient India differs much from the casteism based upon heredity. In the Varna system, a Brahmin gets respect if he has acquired knowledge and imparts it to other. A *Sudra* can become a Brahmin if he gains knowledge and proficiency. Changes of *Varna* and *inter-varna* marriages were permissible. This is entirely different from the caste system of the medieval and modern period in which the criterion of heredity determines one's caste.

The medieval period was characterized by the tendencies such as the brahminism, fatalism, casteism and authoritarianism. Literatures of this period have scribes regarding the supremacy of the priestly class degrading the status of lower classes and women. The schools of Lokayata, Buddhism and Jainism which sprang during medieval period revolted against the priestly hierarchy succeeded to some extent in bringing about some radical changes in the life of the common people. Though they could control the tyranny of the priestly class, because of its extremist attitude regarding the social life, they could not sustain. The hedonistic philosophy of Charvaka which aimed at the pleasure here on earth was not taken seriously by thinkers at large. Jainism and Buddhism fought against most of the social mal practices and evils and could induce a positive impact in the social life of common masses. But these social movements failed to root out the many of the hideous customs and manners of the higher classes. It was in the sway of Gupta and Rajput rule, the priestly classes tried to restore their lost hypocrisy. The emergence of innumerable caste and sub caste and the rigidity of social and moral codes prevailed during the period had proved an impediment to the social progress of the country. In those days social evils like sati, child marriage, untouchability, bigamy etc., had all matured and had taken monstrous proportion. They stood in the way of unity and development in the Indian social milieu and continued till the early twentieth century. Rigid group of fanatic Hindus exerted their efforts to preserve social determinism and had opposed all forms of change. A group of men who were depressed by the existing disastrous social order immediately took to the English culture and were fascinated by the scientific and economic development of the West. With the establishment of the British rule in India, there seems to have grown among Indians a sense that modernization connotes westernization. While there is nothing wrong in learning a language, but blind imitation of an alien cultural frame work only succeeds in creating cultural amalgam that will be the centre of power because of his borrowed kudos. Thus the British rule had damaged the spiritual foundation of Indian society undermining its overall development. This had dragged the country in perpetual cultural ruination and helpless dependence on others which is inimical to true nationalism and creative genius.

Another group of thinkers separated from two aforesaid groups of social determinists and social dynamists tried a comfortable compromise between the two extremes of conservation and radicalism that forms the main content of modern social thought. The British influence on education, administration and the society including religion's influence also contributed to the rise of such movements. These English-educated Indians had made a criticism on orthodox groups' obsession with pollution and ritualism and had attempted to distinguish the essence of Hinduism from its historical accretion and had interpreted those as extrinsic to true religion and as even wrong.[20] They advocated a synthesis between Indian culture with that of the West by opposing any kind of dogmatic inflexibility where religion is concerned and also objected to be slaves of science and western ideals. The renaissance movement in the nineteenth century which emerged with intention of the upheaval of the weaker sections of the society was a result of this group. Many socio-religious reform movements, initiated by different social and religious organization, were started for improving the socio-cultural conditions of the people without neglecting the essential spiritual ideals that India had always cherished.

---

[20] M.N.Srinivas, *Social Change in Modern India* (New Delhi: Orient Blackswan Private Limited, 2009), p.131.

Most of the reform movements that emerged during the renaissance period had the definite aim of improving the social, cultural and religious situation in the country. As a natural consequence of the aspiration to revive India's ancient glory and greatness, these movements laid stress on socially useful action along with knowledge and interpretation of the tradition.

Brahma Samaj was the first reform movement started by Raja Ram Mohan Roy left a deep impression upon contemporary social, political and religious milieu. The principles of the society evaded all rigidities, stressed the importance of universal brotherhood and equality and the existence of a single God, and thereby tried to revive the people of India from the slumber of superstition and spiritual apathy. In the religious field, it wanted to restore Hindu religion to its original purity. It did not reject absolutely the observance of religious rites and ceremonies but simply showed that they were not indispensable. But it raised criticism against the practice of priestly hypocrisy, idol worship, elaborate rituals and sacrifices. In the social sphere it stood against all inequalities, child marriage, sati, bigamy, caste discrimination and the rest of the problems that beset the Indian society by presenting the precepts of Jesus as well as the treasures of the Upanisads. Another important contribution of the Samaj was the promotion of widow remarriage and its emphasis on women education. After Ram Mohan Roy, the Samaj was further propagated by such great figures as Debendranath Tagore and Kesab Chandra Sen. It later broke into two groups on account of differences in basic principles resulting in the formation of the Adi Brahma Samaj led by Tagore and the Brahma Samaj under the leadership of Kesab Chandra

Sen. The former introduced the spirit of rationalism in its members and gave emphasis on subjective authority of intuition instead of accepting the authority of Vedas. Its aim was to make worship part of every one's life, a worship not made through superstitious religious norms, but a prayer suggested and advocated by reason and intelligence. The latter was described as "Human Catholicism" [21] because of its synthetic approach towards various religions. Its consummation of various religious concepts like the fatherhood of God and the brotherhood of man leaves great impact on Indian social milieu. The Society, in social issues, was no less revolutionary than Ram Mohan Roy's Brahma Samaj.

Prarthana Samaj, under the leadership of M.G.Ranade was an institution which aimed at the declared objectives of the disapproval of caste, the introduction of widow-marriage, promotion of female education and abolition of child marriage. Ranade was of the opinion that as a man's political life depends on his social environment, the social freedom was more important than the political freedom. The best way of social reform was in fact to go to the root of various problems and to take away their basic causes. Ranade set forth that the isolation and submission to outward force or power more than to the inward conscience, perception of factitious difference between men and men on the basis of birth, passive acquiescence in evil or wrong doing, and a general indifference to secular wellbeing and believing in fatalism as the

---

[21] Dr. Nirmala Tandon, *op.cit.*, p.28.

primary causes of all social evils.[22] Therefore he wanted to root out the above said erroneous attitudes and tried to flourish the ideals of fraternity, submission to the power of conscience, equality of men, and active interest in secular affairs thereby giving utmost importance to social matters.

Arya Samaj led by Dayananda Saraswathy aimed at the revival of Indian society in the light of accepted ideas of old, since it accepted Vedas as the base for all social and religious changes. Unlike Brahma Samaj and Prarthana Samaj which admitted the acceptance of many western ideals, the Samaj fastened itself to the omniscience of the Vedas. He analysed that being cut from the genuine source of truth was the cause of the pitiable condition of Indians. He held that the Vedas which upholds the message of unity had nothing in it to support class or caste discrimination. Besides the Samaj stood for the emancipation of women and vehemently criticized the practice of child marriage, sati, the extravagance of marriage expenses, denial of female education and other customs that impede the social progress.

Sri Ramakrishna unlike other great reformers of the nineteenth century was not primarily interested in social reformation. He was concerned with personal realization as he was convinced of the fact that society would be cleansed of its evils if the minds of the people were enlightened by pure religious ideas. Hence he advised that man should first be purged of all egoism and should do social service as a part of

---

[22] M.G.Ranade, *Religious Reform and Social reform: A Collection of Essays and Speeches* Collected and compiled by M.B.Kolasker,G.Claridge and Co.,1902, p.172. Cited in Dr. Nirmala Tandon, *op.cit.*, p.30.

divine service.[23] Thus one might argue that it was Ramakrishna and his disciple Vivekananda who for the first time presented a social philosophy which has its base in spirituality.[24] Sri Ramakrishna, before his passing away, had formed a new Order of monks out of his young disciples, with Vivekananda as their leader. The Order had decided itself to carry out the responsibility to preserve and enhance the deep spirituality and the spirit of universality which found prominence in the life and teachings of the Master. Vivekananda added to the inward spiritual life of the Order, an outward programme of cultural and humanitarian activities in the name of his Master came to be known as the Ramakrishna Math and the Ramakrishna Mission. It was Vivekananda who gave the movement the inspiring motto: *Atmano mokshartham jagadhitaya ca*- 'for the freedom of oneself and for the welfare of the world. It was with the dual purpose of contemplation and social action, that Ramakrishna Mission was established. Till then many of the notable names in India were accustomed either to follow frantically Indian spirituality and its cultural heritage or to stick on to western rationalism blindly which resulted in a kind of despiritualization and denationalization. But the idea of bringing about a synthesis between the Eastern thoughts and the Western ideals had not clearly emanated until Vivekananda brought it out. Thus by the setting up of Ramakrishna Mission, Vivekananda intended to follow not only the tradition of mysticism and devotion, but also the ideas of Western

---

[23] T.M.P.Mahadevan, *Outlines of Hinduism* (Bombay: Chetana Ltd.,1960), p.222-3.
[24] V. Sukumaran Nair, *Swami Vivekananda: The Educator* (NewDelhi: Sterling Publishers Pvt. Ltd., 1987), p. 14.

philanthropy and social welfare programmes.[25] The Mission rendered service in the fields of education, public health, rural development, religious harmony and inculcation of moral values. It represents a fine synthesis of eastern and western ideals of philosophy of history and culture, concepts of nationalism, humanism, tolerance and freedom.

Evolution of Indian Social Thought -From Ancient to the Modern Period

As social philosophy is not an understanding of physical or geo-political records, it is not so simple to comprehend it without knowing about its context. Social philosophy of modern period is not an exception to this phenomenon. The task of a social philosopher lies in exposing the contradictions that prevailed in the society, to arouse the consciousness and ethos of the people to do away with the perplexing social situation that generates, permits and perpetuate such a state of affairs, finding out its root causes and to evolve an ideology that could bring about radical changes in the society by preserving social values existing in that society. The situation that prevailed in the nineteenth century India necessitates the philosophers of the age to think that it was futile to isolate themselves from the social realities under the garb of abstract thinking with no relation to social situation. They realized that the philosophy in that phase of crisis cannot be integrated with living under historical conditions alone, but it must point out direction of change and emancipation; otherwise it will have to be subordinate to the status quo or the vested interest of a few. Philosophy involves being as well as living. Its value is not merely intellectual, not merely to

---

[25] Dr. Kalidas Nag, *"Swami Vivekananda,"* PrabuddhaBharata, 47(1942), p. 15.

stimulate thought, but also to guide action. Its ideas and ideals are not left suspended in transcendental level, as it was unable to come down to earth in practical and practicable form. Hence the modern social thinkers have highlighted the ideal of human unity and love and applied it in the secular realm. And in doing all this, every form of invidious distinction on the basis of caste, creed, sex, colour, economic class must be made their target of attack. The philosopher in the society is the person to point out the fact that human identity and development is attainable through mutual trust, understanding and love and not through exploitation and dehumanization. Man's species identity can be best manifested in a society free from the vices mentioned above and the philosopher can give direction to social movement through constant rational analysis of the practices of the society, its observation to anti-man ideology.

As the ancient Indian philosophy interprets world as an imposition upon the spirit it prescribes social service only as a potent means of self-realisation and god-realisation. Thus not only in metaphysics but in axiology too Indian spiritualism leads to negation of social philosophy by degrading social service as means and not an end in itself.[26] In accordance with the ancient scriptures they proclaim that if one wants to achieve his own welfare, he must strive to ensure the welfare of other human beings. Certain expressions like '*Vasudaiva Kudumbakam*', '*Sarvebhavatu sukhinah*' and '*Sahanavavatu sahanou bhunakthu saha viryam kara vavahai*' in the scriptures of Upanishads and in the Gita reveals that our tradition itself has the seed of this genuine, robust humanism which stands for the unity of whole of humanity and need

---

[26] Ramnath Sharma, *op.cit.*, p.26.

for the fellow-feeling among men. But these teachings which are confined only in theory have brought it to the focal point of our thinking and action by the modern thinkers of India. The Gita exhortation of cherishing and serving each other for the highest general welfare (*lokasamgraha*) also has a similar intent. A similar view is also presented by the German philosopher Immanuel Kant in his 'Metaphysics of Morals': "So act as to treat humanity whether in thine own person or in that of any other in every case as an end without, never as means only".[27] These great thoughts were meant for developing a society that is conducive to the ultimate happiness of all. These ideals can only be justified if it inspires its votaries to a wise altruistic and untiring activity, both in self development and social development.

The contemporary Indian thinker, in a like manner, upholds that it is the duty of every soul as such, i.e., as gods, which applied to the society as a whole. This revival in metaphysical thinking could effect a drastic change on the entire world of thoughts including social, political, economic, religious and spiritual.[28] The contemporary thinkers while trying to revive the old vedic and the upanisadic thoughts wanted to maintain a continuation of the modern renaissance in Indian philosophy. Thus contemporary social philosophy with its monistic, idealistic and integral approach dealt not only philosophical thinking, but also multi-sided life involving religious as well as intense activity in social and political fields. They made service to mankind not as a mean but as an end in itself.

---

[27] Barbara Mackimon, Andrew Fiala, *Ethics: Theory and Contemporary Issues* (United States: Cengage Learning, 2009), p.131.
[28] Dr.Ramnath Sharma, *op cit*, p.27

The integral characteristic of Indian social thought of contemporary period include instructive methods in philosophy, integral vision of human personality, harmony of nationalism and the meeting of extremes in thought and these are all in line with the ages old philosophical tradition of the land.[29] Every thought has to become broad till it covers the entire world. Every aspiration must go on increasing till it has engulfed the whole of humanity may the whole life within its scope.[30] Spinoza in the nineteenth century also conveyed the same thought when he says the greatest good as an expression of the idea of union which the mind has with the whole of nature. He has stated that the more the mind knows the better it understands the forces and the order of nature, the better the mind will be capable to direct itself and lay down rules for itself.[31] Many great social thinkers, both of the East and of the West have preserved this thought of balance between the body and the spirit and between man as part of nature and man as part of society.

Objectives of the Study

The major objective of the thesis includes understanding the social pertinence of the philosophy of Vivekananda. It aims to analyse how he applied the highly abstract metaphysical theory of Vedanta to facilitate social cohesion by proclaiming the spiritual solidarity of man. An attempt is made to trace out the major concepts and principles regarding the society in relation to moral, cultural and spiritual values. It also examines how the thought promotes raising the standard of living of the lower

---

[29] *ibid.*, p.30.
[30] *The Complete Works of Swami Vivekanada*, Vol.3, p.226.
[31] Jawaharlal Nehru, *op cit.*, p.561.

classes, high level of universal education, women's equality and empowerment, universal religion and see how these thoughts lead to some practical suggestions which can give a healthy rethinking and reorientation to our approach to many peculiar problems plaguing the Indian society. It aims to analyse the approach of dialectical complementarities of the theory and practice, tradition and modernity, sacred and the secular, man and woman, the educated as well as the ignorant which he adopted while dealing with social thinking.

Review of Literature

It is true that a good number of research works have been carried out regarding Vivekananda's ideas and message. Despite the passage of a century people's interest on his life and work in still intact, may be increasing perhaps because the problems and issues he has so forcefully raised in the last decade of nineteenth century remained unresolved and needs attention even today. Besides, his ideas have its base on certain lively eternal truths and one can never find a note of despair in his utterances. He gave to humanity a message of hope and a vision which is too precious to be forgotten. In the preparation of this thesis the nine volumes of the Complete Works of Swami Vivekananda form the primary resources. Apart from that the recent literature on Vivekananda has also been thoroughly read and discussed. Vivekananda's messages are scattered all over the pages of his works and is not so palpably clear to casual readers. Therefore an attempt is made to present all the excerpts on this subject on a systematized form, believing that in this study in the modern context of social re-thinking will be highly beneficial.

Methodology

The methodology followed in the preparation of this thesis is mainly descriptive. Social philosophy, its very nature and goal is espoused in the background of Vivekananda's thoughts. It is analytic also since social ideas are analysed in detail. A synthesis of the metaphysical with the social, is yet another methodology used.

Significance of the Study

The trend towards globalization that had the prospect of bringing about global peace and shared affluence has instead, greatly increased inequality, injustice and economic disparity and exploitation. By paying least heed to the inner nature, man has activated a chain of reaction such as alienation from reality, from nature, and from his own true self. As a result he has lost sight of the highest aspiration of the unity of human kind through love, compassion and democratic equality. He needs to be confronted with conflicts of worldly values and faith, between economically developed and the under developed societies, between generations, between religions, between reason and dogma, between gender and so on.

Against the background of these lifeless and petrified developments, Vivekananda's philosophy seems more relevant today than ever before. The thought gives a new connotation to the philosophical thinking by combining the socio-political and the ethico-spiritual ideas aiming at an all-round development of man, both inwardly and outwardly. It tries to espouse the lofty spiritual heights with the plains of the phenomenal world, encompassing the truth that the spirit without matter is empty and matter devoid of spirit is blind. The spiritual messages of oneness of existence, unity of faiths, and the divinity of the soul in the primal cultural tradition are applied adroitly in an authentic way for the reconstructions of society. The vital principles of spiritual solidarity and spiritual democracy seen throughout his thought exhorts man to perceive the same divine self in each and all, not only in nature, but in the family, in the society, and in the state. This in turn aids him to cast-off the essential difference between a man and a man leading to a peaceful and harmonious society. The more a person realises the oneness of all, the better for him, if fails to realise it he turns his face towards destruction which form the keynote of the teachings of Vivekananda. It nullifies the difference between the one and the many, i.e., the individual and the society. The happiness of one depends on the happiness of all and the wellbeing of all depends upon the wellbeing of one. This paves the way for interdependence and interconnectivity of life. Through this thought each man is called upon to strive not only for one's own individual happiness and emancipation, but also for social and community welfare. Thus his thought showed the path of infinite freedom from man's tiny egocentric self beyond the limits of all selfishness. In it, the metaphysical ideals are be suitably presented in a positivistic and pragmatic form for overcoming human separateness, religious conflicts, social and economic disparities which our society is now facing.

Layout of the Thesis

The work is divided into five chapters. The first chapter is an introduction discussing the relevance of social thought in philosophy, how society can be changed in accordance with the social ideals and values. It also contains a description of ancient, medieval and modern social situations that prevailed in India and also the thoughts of these different periods in Indian social milieu.

The second chapter presents in broad outline an authentic account of such aspects of his wonderful life, versatile mind and manifold activities which imprint a vivid image of him, serving as an inspiration to everyone to lead a higher and nobler life. The life and thoughts of Vivekananda were the products of multiple influences spread over many years of many thoughts. An attempt is being made in this chapter to examine the various social, cultural and intellectual factors that shaped the philosophy of Vivekananda. The influence of his family, the knowledge acquired from his reading on both oriental and occidental thoughts, his interaction with people from different backgrounds and events from his own experience forms the main content of the chapter. It also describes the main incidents in his life, bringing out as far as possible his ideas and ideals, messages and teachings; so far they are associated with those incidents.

In the third chapter, a reconciliation of Dvaita, Visistadvaita and Advaita as stages of spiritual ascension is being discussed. A description of the basic metaphysical principle of the Vedanta including the concepts of *Brahman, Iswara, jagat, Maya* are also given. This chapter also deals with the four yogic practices- *karma, jnana, bhakti* and *raja* – in relation to discover the divine nature or oneness of human beings. With a strong base on the metaphysics of Advaita, here, his exposition of neo-Vedanta is being made which relates man to man, man to god and extracting a single philosophy of seeing and serving god in man. Hence his philosophy explores a great message of inter-dependence and mutual service.

The fourth chapter examines how he churned out a simple and socially applicable philosophy from the abstract ideals of Vedanta and applied it in the context of family and social life. Here secular and the spiritual are not kept in water-tight compartments and every subject affecting human life, thought and action which received his keen attention is discussed in this chapter. Broad and deep aspects of his thought including spiritualism, universal values, religion, spirit of service, education, character-building, emancipation of women and masses and many other issues of social interest are held in discussion in this chapter. His philosophy of *karma-sannyasa* is revealed here by his dexterity in synthesizing tradition and with modernity, material advancement and spiritual development and best of the East and of the West, individual development with social progress.

The fifth chapter along with highlighting the summary of the thesis gives an evaluation of his social ideas. The solution offered on various social problems with his acute observation and deep insights are also applicable to various social problems that we observe in our own current social context. It was the acute observation, critical reflection and deep insight on many social issues that he puts on them made it relevant in every areas for all time.

The thoughts of Vivekananda ever remained as a rare combination of intellectual eminence and humane disposition. Throughout the thought there prevailed an attitude that surpasses the self and encompasses the ambience of fellowmen in a spirit of communion. It is not a mere system of ideals comprising epistemology, metaphysics, ethics and soteriology. On the other hand it encapsulates questions about social life and interpretations of society and social institutions in terms of ethical and spiritual values to further the well-being of mankind as a whole. It contains humanistic, socialistic as well as spiritualistic elements that surpass the self and encompass the ambience of fellowmen in a spirit of communion with the entire humanity.

CHAPTER – II

SOCIO-CULTURAL BACKGROUND OF THE PHILOSOPHY OF VIVEKANANDA

It is natural for those raised on limited conceptions of life, to limit their thoughts to a particular group or a particular area on this planet, as it is natural for those nurtured on diverse influences to widen their vision and service into world comprehension and world fellowship. They do not herd themselves behind barriers of any particular sect and separate themselves from the rest of mankind, as for him the oneness of mankind is a fact and not a fable. His philosophy is based on the idea of universal doctrine and culture that aimed at developing a society, wherein individual, nation and the world without losing their identities, find their ultimate harmony and unity. His larger and nobler vision feels himself as a citizen of the world-community. The life and thoughts of Vivekananda were the products of multiple influences spread over many years of many thoughts. There are various factors, the social, cultural and intellectual influences that shaped his life and philosophy. It includes the influence of his relations, the information acquired from his reading of both oriental and occidental thoughts, his communication with people from different backgrounds and events from his own experience. It describes the main incidents in his life, his ideas and ideals, messages and teachings associated with those incidents. It might be because of these varied and multiple influences he could design a synthetic approach that proposed to develop unity out of diversities, coherence out of incoherence throughout his thought process. His thought remains a comprehensive one synthesizing tradition and modernity, spiritual and secular, encompassing the ideas of the East and of the West.

The Social Milieu of Vivekananda's Thought

The thought and personality of every man is in large part reflections of the society in which he lives. Individuals acquire their knowledge, skills, customs, ideals and morals from their social environment.[1] The social being of man determines his thought.[2] His attitudes and values are predominantly affected by the existing social order and even by the past social traditions, customs and manners. The life and philosophy of Vivekananda is not an exception to this view. It is characterised as the fusion of sociality with spirituality interpreting the traditional Indian thoughts of Vedanta to suit the modern Indian mind. The first segment of the chapter namely, the social background consists of milieu in which Vivekananda grew up and worked, his family backdrop, the period and place in which he lived, his mental makeup, his scientific education, and his knowledge of men and things all over the world.

---

[1] K. Satchidananda Murthy, *Evolution of Indian Philosophy* (New Delhi: D.K. Print World (P) Ltd., 2007), p. 53.

[2] Marx and Engels, *Selected Works* (Moscow: Progress Publishers, 1969), Vol.1, p.300.

Parental Influences

The family is a basic or fundamental form of society, the first place where an individual is socialized.³ It is in the family that he learns the various methods of living, behaviour, conversation etc. In the case of Vivekananda also family plays a dominant role in his socialization. The basic nature of Vivekananda was moulded by two divergent poles of pious religiosity from his mother and an agnostic inclined intellectualism from his father.⁴ Thus the principles that derive from his parents played a significant role in his character formation. The first and the deepest influence in the life of a child is surely its mother. Narendranath was no exception to this universal law. Round the Hindu epics the Ramayana and the Mahabharata saturated with popular Hinduism, his mother wove the pattern of his life.⁵ Her strong moral and religious instruction about the stories of Hindu deities made a great impact on Vivekananda's future life and in shaping his moral values. Actually the classics of the world reveal to one of the variety of human nature in all its intensity and pathos. So the study of them definitely helped Narendranath understand human nature and thereby made him adopt a tolerant, sympathetic and understanding outlook. He commented that the philosophy propounded in the Ramayana and the Mahabharata

---

³ Dr. R.N. Sharma, *Social Control and Social Change* (Merit: Rajhans Prakashan Mandir, 1979), p.22.

⁴ S.J. Thomas Mannumel, *The Advaita of Vivekananda* (Madras: J.R. Publications Pvt. Ltd., 1991), p.11.

⁵ M.L. Ahuja, *Glimpses of some Great Indians* (New Delhi: Vikas Publishing House Pvt. Ltd., 1997), p.148.

are enriched with grand ideas and they do not depend upon any single personality which he conceived as the most significant trait exclusive to Hinduism.[6] It shows his appreciation towards the ancient scriptures and Indian spiritualism which his mother had inculcated. Thus his mother played a decisive role in developing deep religiosity and moral values in the young Narendranath.

Vivekananda imbibed the humanistic and rationalistic attitude of his father which later helped him to transform himself into a philosopher with a socialistic view point. Though he had a religious mind he never had any blind love for traditions and did not swallow any superstitions. This is because of the influence of his father who maintained a rational outlook throughout his life. His father Viswanath Datta had led a sceptical life and he had doubts regarding the existence of the soul or life after death.[7] Discussions, arguments and counter arguments with a large circle of friends were a regular feature in his house. According to his biography, Vivekananda had the opportunity to participate in scholarly discussions and it is from that liberal and literary atmosphere young Narendranath learnt the art of reasoning.[8] He was free from dogmatism and sectarian exclusiveness and did not adhere to the social rules and

---

[6] SwamiVivekananda, *The Complete Works of SwamiVivekananda* (Kolkata: Advaita Ashrama, 2003), Vol.4, pp.75-6.

[7] Romain Rolland, *The Life of Ramakrishna* (Calcutta : Advaita Ashrama, 1975), pp. 222-3.

[8] Ajeet Jawed, *Swami Vivekananda – An Iconoclastic Ascetic* (New Delhi : Ane Books India, 2007), p.23.

practices blindly.[9] Many a time he questioned the validity behind such practices and tried to breach them to see the consequent effects. It was the great influences from deeply religious mother and a rational-minded father during his tender years that sowed in him the seeds of deep spiritualism and morality as well as a humanistic and socialistic outlook.

Another important personality that had impact upon his life was of his grandfather Durga Charan Datta. He renounced the world in search of God and became a monk at the age of twenty. This incident made Vivekananda to realise the significance of monastic life that even in his childhood he boldly proclaimed that he would become a *Sannyasin*.[10] But unlike his grandfather for him *sannyasa* was not an other-worldly pilgrimage, but a social journey in this world for the upliftment of his society. Society and social problems ever remained in him as a personal issue which created in him a kind of self-sacrificing attitude to liberate society from bondage. This brief account of his early life shows how his parents moulded his personality to construct his philosophy of life.

The Impact of Education

The rational outlook which Vivekananda imbibed from his father was further strengthened by the scientific and secular education which he had received. Both in

---

[9] P. Ramakrishnan, *SwamiVivekananda – Awakener of Modern India* (Chennai : Ramakrishna Matt), p.16.

[10] Eastern and Western Disciples, *The Life of Swami Vivekananda*, (Calcutta : AdvaitaAshrama, 1974), p.4.

school and in college, he was known for his radical views. His study of both modern and ancient texts was vast and his capability of drawing apt practical lesson from them was unparalleled. The early education at the Metropolitan institute of Iswar Chandra Vidya Sagar prepared the ground for the study of his favourite subjects like Sanskrit, English and History, especially the History of India. His learning on the philosophies of Herbert Spencer, Immanuel Kant, Aurther Schopenhaur, August Comte and J.S. Mill had produced a strong effect on his mind.[11] Mill's 'Three Essays on Religion' perturbed his theistic mind. He stated that holding an atheistic position by following reason is better than blind belief in two hundred million gods on the authority of anybody.[12] Focussing on reason, he held the view that science has every right to question religion and to discard what is illogical and superstitious in it. However, he was aware of the fact that reason cannot infringe on phenomena outside its group. Though religion is beyond the reach of reason, one cannot get at the sphere of spirituality in the absence of reason. Vivekananda says that no genuine inspiration ever contradicts reason.[13] He recognises the reasoning power of man a good deal although he states that though there is something higher than intellect, the way that leads is through the intellect.[14] Hence he handles both reason and religion as supplementary rather than incompatible. He would rather require that "Science

---

[11] S.S. Mittal, *The Social and Political Ideas of Swami Vivekananda* (New Delhi: B.V. Gupta for Metropolitan Book Co. Pvt. Ltd., 1979), p.22.

[12] Jawaharlal Nehru, *The Discovery of India*, Calcutta : Oxford University Press, 1999), p. 188.

[13] *ibid.*, p. 187

[14] *The Complete Works of SwamiVivekananda*, Vol. 8, p. 20.

should get spiritualised and religion get rationalized".[15] As a true Vedantin, he had no quarrel with science and civilization. In short, the education that he had received at school and college furthered the depth of his understanding of Eastern and Western thoughts and made him aware of the general pathetic situation of the Indian social system which was under the clutches of foreign rule and of the tyranny of priestly class.

The Influence of Sri Ramakrishna and His Teachings

It was Vivekananda's scepticism and the search for God took that him to Sri Ramakrishna Parama Hamsa. He alone had replied affirmatively to Narendranath when asked about God's existence.[16] The meeting had kindled in him the final determination to follow the path he himself had trodden, because in SriRamakrishna, Narendranath found his highest ideal realised.[17] The five years of discipleship under Sri Ramakrishna were formative for the mind of Narendranath which transformed him into Swami Vivekananda. Many of his speeches and writings explore the great respect and reverence he had for his teacher. He regarded him not only a man of realisation, but a person who can transmit spirituality and possessed the strength to keep the bounds of society intact.[18] He said that those who live in God cannot take a harsh view of the misfits or the failures of society and have full compassion for and full

---

[15] B.R. Rajam Aiyer, *Rambles of Vedanta* (Madras :S. Ganesan Publishers, 1925), p.4.

[16] *The Complete Works of Swami Vivekananda*, Vol. 5, p.186

[17] Daine Collinson and Robert Wilkinson, *Thirty Five Oriental Philosophers* (London: Routledge, 1994), p.82.

[18] *The Complete Works of Swami Vivekananda*, Vol. 4, p. 28.

understanding of all the ills to which a human being is subjected.[19] It was about Sri Ramakrishna that Vivekananda upheld the above observation.

The role of Ramakrishna Paramahamsa in bringing up in Vivekananda a deep-rooted interest in the Vedanta and concern for the service of society is crucial. It was the highest spiritual ideal to realise God and to live in the service of humankind that had inspired Narendranath to dedicate his life to humanity. When the young Narendranath expressed his wish to remain continually absorbed in a super conscious state his master was displeased and had given him the advice that he was not meant to only taste the bliss of God for himself, but had to share it with others.[20] Thus it was the great humanist Sri Ramakrishna that entrusted in Narendranath the great task of giving shelter to the suffering mankind by saying thus: "Naren, today I have given you my all and have become a Fakir, a penniless beggar. By the force of power transmitted by me, great things will be done by you; only after that you will go to whence you came."[21] All the advice and admonition of Sri Ramakrishna made a great change regarding Vivekananda's views of life and he wishes to take the enormous responsibility of providing shelter to mankind against the scorching miseries of the world. His master's emphasis on service to man had a very great impact on him.

---

[19] *idem.*

[20] His Eastern and Western Disciples, *op.cit.*, Vol.1, p.162.

[21] V.K.R.V.Rao, *Swami Vivekananda*, p.45. cited in P.R.Bhuyan, *Swami Vivekananda: Messiah of Resurgent India*,(NewDelhi: Atlantic Publishers and Distributors, 2003), p.8.

Through his life Sri Ramakrishna proved that sanctity is not unworldliness.[22] It is participation in the agony of the world with a proper frame of mind, realising that it is the same God that indwells in all sentient beings. This great message is communicated effectively by his master's utterance *'Jiva as Shiva'*. Again Sri Ramakrishna's exhortion that one should not serve others on account of mercy, but service should be done in a manner of worship to God has greatly appealed Vivekananda's philosophy of service. Realisation of divinity in humanity leaves no room for egoism, realizing this man cannot feel jealousy or pity for any other being. Hence he does not stand exclusive among the founders of religion like Lord Buddha and Jesus Christ who never deserted the drunkards, the prostitutes, the thieves and all the sinners of the world. Hence he suggested that mental renunciation is far superior to physical renunciation or running away from the social life.

Two great ideas that shine in Sri Ramakrishna's life and message are deepening of man's spiritual life and the resulting selfless service to the human world. To the young men destined to be monks he pointed out the steep path of renunciation, both external and internal. They must take the vow of absolute continence and eschew all thought of greed and lust. By the practice of continence the aspirants develop a subtle nerve through which they understand the deeper mysteries of God. For them self control is final, imperative and absolute. The *sanyasins* are the teachers of men and their lives should be totally free from blemish. The Master selected his

---

[22] William Radice, *Swami Vivekananda and Modernisation of Hinduism* (Calcutta Oxford University Press, 1998), p. 266.

future monks from young men untouched by lust or wealth and fit enough to be cast in his spiritual mould.

Another significant utterance of Ramakrishna which throws a flood of light on Vivekananda about the relative positions of dualism, qualified non-dualism, and pure non-dualism had much influenced his philosophy is as follows: "Rama worshipped as a divine incarnation asked his faithful devotee Hanuman, as how the latter looked the former. Hanuman replied: when I consider myself as a physical being, thou are the master and I am the servant. When I consider myself as an individual being, thou are the whole, and I am one of thy parts. And when I realize myself as the Atman, I am one with Thee' Hanuman's reply is, thus indicative of the great truth that far from being antagonistic one to the other, dualism, qualified non-dualism and pure non-dualism are but successive steps in spiritual realization – last state is being attained when the aspirant loses all consciousness of individuality in union with God."[23] Sri Ramakrishna accepts the apparently divergent beliefs like the law of Karma, rebirth, incarnation, doctrine of grace, importance of guru, One God as also many gods and goddesses, idol worship and so on. But he is not interested in ritualism and wants non-Brahmins to be initiated in the worship of God. He made an attempt to defend Hindu religious practices on rationalistic ground, but never exhibited any feeling of pride

---

[23] Amiya Kumar Mazumdar, *Rediscovering Vivekananda* (Kolkata: FrontPage, 2011), p.76.

towards Hindu cultural heritage.[24] In fact Ramakrishna did not try to purify Hinduism in the manner of other reformers like Ram Mohan Roy or Dayananda Saraswathi.

Another crux in Ramakrishna's teaching which placed a great impression on Vivekananda is his views on the acceptance of different religious. He keeps on aversion towards all kinds of dogmatism. He does not try to formulate a well-defined and precise type of religion. He never adopts a negative or critical attitude towards any religions but tries to present their positive side – how they could be carried into life and practiced.[25] The very first principle of his ideal is: "If one religion is true, then by the same very logic all other religions are also true, the verification of which is found in the fact that holiness, purity and charity are not the exclusive possession of any church in the world and that every system has produced men and women of the most exalted character." [26] Hence Sri Ramakrishna leaves every religion undisturbed and does no attempt to start a new religion. Instead he wanted to break down the barriers of sectarianism and dogma.[27] He condemns the phrase 'religious-tolerance', and pleaded for the acceptance of different religious. Believing in the unity of all religions he uttered, "Ascension to acceptance and ultimately to absorption of other

---

[24] D.R. Jatava, *Evolution of Indian SocialThought* (Jaipur: Bohra Publication, 1987), p.187.

[25] *The Complete Works of SwamiVivekananda*,Vol. 5 p, 190.

[26] *The Complete Works of SwamiVivekananda*,Vol. 1 p, 22.

[27] *The Complete Works of Swami Vivekananda*,Vol. 5, p. 186.

faiths was the goal of true religion". [28] All diverse modes of worship are agreeable to God. He himself traversed the various paths of the Hindu faith and also lived the life of a pious Christian and a devout Muslim and attained perfection in each. Through all these experiments, he realized that the truth that all religions are at bottom one. To fight to assume antagonistic attitude is the exact contradictory of his teachings which dwells on the truth that the world is moved by love.[29] Thus yet another mission of his master which Vivekananda imbibed is the realization of fundamental unity underlying all religions.

Again, Sri Ramakrishna holds that individual has meaning only as a social unit, and a society has existence only as a group of individuals. He looked at the individual in the succession of other individuals in society as they are inseparable from each other. And he wanted that a spiritual seeker must be extremely alive in this truth. In fact the very base of spirituality is the realisation of identity between the individual and everything else through God, the supreme Spirit. Vivekananda found that the best in Hinduism is personified in the practical living form in the life of Ramakrishna Paramahamsa. He wrote about his master's message to the modern world thus : "Do not care for doctrines, do not care for dogmas, or sects, or churches or temple, they count for little compared with the essence of existence in each man which is spirituality and the more this is developed in man the more powerful is he for good".[30]

---

[28] Nemai Sadhan Bose, *Swami Vivekananda* (NewDelhi:Sahithya Academy,1994), p.13.

[29] *The Complete Works of SwamiVivekananda*, Vol. 4, pp. 418-9.

[30] *The Complete Works of Swami Vivekananda*, Vol.4, p. 187.

In short his message was one of love, service, renunciation and religions harmony. He wanted the devout disciple to have a sense of mission to pass his message to the world at large. He said that he was willing to suffer all sorts of bodily pain and death, a hundred thousand times, if the act could bring a single soul to freedom and salvation.[31] The acts of social service for him are not something that one engages out of compassion. Though Ramakrishna was not directly concerned with any social reconstruction, but his life itself was a service.

Cultural Background of Vivekananda's Thought

The historical facts, cultural conditions and the environmental pressures of Vivekananda's age acted in him as an inner force that helped to shape his thoughts and ideals. The ideological and overall scenario in India of his period was pathetic to the extreme, it was disorderly confused and chaotic, primarily ecclesiastical and superstitious. Vivekananda wanted a dynamic change in his own country and the world over.[32] He was not willing to retreat from his responsibility on the presumption that the historical conditions dictate the pattern of society. On the other hand he set his face in the right direction and had dejected what is harmful to Indian social milieu. The lack of social freedom and inadequate preparation for change, he observed are the causes of material and ideological penury among the ordinary people of India. Social

---

[31] Max Muller, *Ramakrishna : His life and Sayings* (London : Longmans Green and Co., 1898), p.57.

[32] A.V. Rathna Reddy, *Political Philosophy of Swami Vivekananda* (New Delhi : Sterling Publishers Pvt. Ltd.,1984), p. 56.

determination remains definitely a check for the individual and social growth. Vivekananda ideas on social freedom and equality, his defence of individual rights and attack on social privileges clearly show his approach against social determination. For the progress of any society dynamism is more important than stability and order. Therefore Vivekananda had warned that if Indian society remains stagnant with antiquated beliefs, prejudices and caste rigidities causing a situation of confusion and primitivism, it might hamper its social progress.[33]

The speeches and writings of Vivekananda reflect his knowledge and interest in India's history and culture. He is influenced and inspired by the thoughts of ancient India. He observed that though the simple democratic life which prevailed in the ancient India was perplexed due to the migration of the Aryans, their contact with the Indian natives had led to a considerable assimilation of culture on both sides.[34] *Varnashrama dharma* and *purusharthas* imposed by the Aryans, really had a superior intention of making one rise higher and higher in proportion to one's learning and culture.[35] But this *varnashrama* system later on turned into a philosophy of social determination and theological fatalism[36] with its rigid rules censoring any growth possibility. The medieval period dominated by casteism, Brahmanism, fanaticism and

---

[33] *ibid.*, p. 57.

[34] Swami Vivekananda, *State, Society and Socialism* (Kolkata: Advaita Ashrama, 2008), p.4.

[35] *The Complete Works of Swami Vivekananda*, Vol. 5, p. 537.

[36] S. Radhakrishnan, *The Hindu View of Life* (1927, rpt, Bombay: George Allen and Unwin (India) Pvt. Ltd.,1976), pp.17-8.

fatalism was detrimental to free intellectual activity. The people who were frustrated with this social situation arose with a tide of social Protestantism. Charvaka, Jainism and Buddhism revolted against the extreme orthodoxy of Vedic religion. Vivekananda supports the sarcasm the Charvaka had on the mere utterance of meaningless syllables without the filling up of social wants.[37] He also appreciates the Jain revolution which took its stand against the ritualistic ceremonialism with its animal and other sacrifices.[38] By virtue of its universal and all-embracing spirit of equality, Vivekananda observed that Buddhism to some extent could deliver the suffering millions of the lower classes from the violent tyrannies of the influential higher castes.[39] But he feels that the idea of 'no-God' of Buddhists had impelled the masses to accept their own gods and devils and hobgoblins which resulted in a tremendous hotchpotch in India.[40] However Vivekananda had high appreciation about Buddha's venture of bringing the religious principles recorded on a bundle of palm leaves to the practical field and applying them in the practical life of the people.

India, a land with a hoary past and rich culture relapsed into obscurity and oblivion and particularly so with the advent of the British. Becoming an appendage of the British empire, it lost in its faith in its pristine values of its own culture and heritage, and started imitating the West. The local population who were fretting in such appalling observances as the child marriage, performance of sati, bigamy,

---

[37] *The Complete Works of Swami Vivekanada* Vol. 4, p. 462.
[38] *idem.*
[39] *idem.*
[40] *The Complete Works of Swami Vivekananda,* Vol. 2, p. 139.

hypocrisy of priests, caste discrimination etc., were lured by the radical views of foreign culture and language and started aping them. The Indian society witnessed the influence of the West in the sixteenth century itself, but it was only in the nineteenth century that it came in direct contact with their rationalistic and scientific thought currents. Until then Indians took it as an honour to be a part of the British empire. It cannot be denied that the contact with the West had widened the mental outlook of the Indians to a considerable extent. The advent of the British impact in education, administration and society including the religious influence through Christian missionaries became a conjoining link between medieval age and modern era. His mind was carried beyond the perilous realm of the senses into the world of intellectuality during this period and he understood the need for empiricism and developed a respect for the western materialistic science and its analytical processes. Vivekananda observes that evil customs like child marriage, polygamy, image worship, sati, and so forth have no place in western religion.[41] Promoting English education, Vivekananda maintains the hope that the spread of western education can root out many evil practices that the priest class had manipulated in Indian society in the name of divine authority. [42] Thus it is by the spread of English education that brought about a general transformation of Indian minds from medievalism to modernism.

---

[41] *The Complete Works of Swami Vivekananda*, Vol. 7, p. 319.
[42] *ibid.*, pp. 172-3.

The spread of English ideals broke the ground for rationalist, humanistic and liberal thought and thereby invigorate an urge for social renaissance among the Indian intellectuals. Regarding the Western influence on Indian minds Hans Kohn writes, "The rising generations assimilated European teachings with astounding receptivity. They quickly became nationalists, democrats and socialist".[43] They started to assimilate the Western ideas and values in all spheres of their lives and enriched themselves. Rational thinking equipped them to evaluate and make an independent judgement on the negative side of the colonial rule and subsequently they began to think about the value of human freedom, sovereignty of the people and the like. The important contribution of the colonial rule was scientific approach to human problems and a critical approach towards socio-religious institutions made them examine the complexity of the Indian situation to find social values relevant to it. These in turn invigorated a critical analysis on their society, economy and government and also to evaluate the true nature of British imperialism in India. So it is an acknowledged fact that the Renaissance in India is an outcome of Western influence.

As encounter with the advanced culture of the Middle East awakened the European mind in the thirteenth and fourteenth centuries, encounter with western culture awakened the Indian mind in the nineteenth century. Vivekananda, spoke on this awakening of India in a lecture delivered in Ramnad a south Indian town: "The longest night seems to be passing away and the sorest trouble seems to be coming to

---

[43] Hans Kohn, *A History of Nationalism in the East*, p.118 cited in P.R.Bhuyan, *Swami Vivekananda: Messiah of Resurgent India* (NewDelhi: Atlantic Publishers and Distributors,2003), p.211.

an end at last and behold, the sleeper is awakening... no outward powers can hold her back any more".[44] This awakening of India was brought about by people separated itself from either of the two aforesaid extremist thoughts - deterministic and dynamistic. These educated ones identifies the wrong principles and ideas which were pulling India back and tried for a revival by advocating a synthesis between Indian culture and the new British ideas. The rise of these great educated people results in various reform movements which paves rejuvenation in the Indian social scenario giving new messages that suit to the needs and conditions of a new age.

Renaissance Period and its Impact

Vivekananda, a product of both Eastern and Western culture, is as much a product of such Indian renaissance as one of its architects. His thoughts exhibit certain traits that are identical with that of western concepts. "Renaissance" it is stated, "is the rebirth or revival of classical learning...to dispel some of the misconceptions long prevalent about the period."[45] It is a drive that tries to understand the ancient with a fresh perspective and to emulate the ancient masters to rejuvenate its life. In the same way, the renaissance of India witnessed a great transformation and revival of interest in its classical culture and thereby instilled a new consciousness and sense of pride for its past glory and greatness of the people of the ancient world.

---

[44] *The Complete Works of Swami Vivekananda,* Vol. 3, pp.145-6.
[45] *Encyclopaedia Britannica,* Vol. 19, p. 123

The Brahma Samaj guided by Ram Mohan Roy, Debendranath Tagore and Kesab Chandra Sen, the AryaSamaj established by Swami Dayananda Saraswathi and the Theosophical movement of his period are the liberal movements that captured the imagination of the educated youths of the country. All these have come under the praise and censure of Vivekananda's pen.

With an intention to rescue Indian society from its degradable condition he joined in the Brahma Samaj. It was his concern for social reform that led Vivekananda to Raja Ram Mohan Roy who later made a deep impression on his religious and social ideas. Deeply versed in Indian thought and as a scholar in Sanskrit, Persian and Arabic, Ram Mohan Roy was a product of the mixed Hindu-Muslim culture. In spite of the impact of Islam and Christianity, he fixed in the foundation of his own faith. He was an earnest-minded investigator of the science of principal religions and critically evaluated them with discrimination and respect. Thus he is renowned as the father of comparative religion as well as the first intellectual syncretised of the spiritual traditions, accepting the positive and liberal and rejecting the negative and dogmatic trends in each.[46] The essential principles of the Samaj, as Vivekananda perceived include avoidance of all rigidity stressing on universal brotherhood and equality, the existence of a single God, were the means to social cohesion.[47] It tried to synthesise ideas from different religions to bring about changes in Indian society. These broad ideas the movement upholds arouse inspiration for

---

[46] Swami Suddhidananda,ed., *Vivekananda as the Turning Point:The Rise of a New Spiritual Wave* (Kolkata: Advaita Ashrama,2013), p. 250.

[47] *The Complete Works of Swami Vivekananda*, Vol. 7, p. 468

Indians to overcome the limitation of localized and isolated life of previous ages. The Brahma Samaj after the death of Ram Mohan Roy had a lean period before its leadership was taken over by Debendranath Tagore who renamed it as Adi Brahma Samaj. Its policy seemed to be *festina lente* paving way for reformation in Hinduism from within, on the basis of a sort of theistic Vedantic intuitionism complemented by an egalitarian ethics.[48] Seeing the movement as partially preoccupied in religious matters and socially unprogressive, a group of men under the leadership of Kesab Chandra Sen left the parent body to form Brahmo Samaj in order to strengthen social service.[49] The Samaj has a distinct church-like character, among the Bengal society it was generally known as "Christianity minus Christ".[50] The leaders of the Samaj espoused the main ideals of Christianity to explore the meaning of Hindu religion. The motto of the Samaj was to break the caste system, encourage widow remarriage and abolish child marriage. Vivekananda maintained a close association with Kesab Chandra Sen and his influences on him cannot be ignored. Later Kesab Chandra Sen was accused of prevarication and authoritarianism on social and religious policy. As a result, a dissident group Sadharan Brahma Samaj broke away in pursuance of their original objectives of social reform. So at the time of Vivekananada, there exist no less than three divisions of the Brahma Samaj, dominating the intellectual scene. Even while carrying the ideological baggage of Kesab's Samaj, Vivekananda left and

---

[48] William Radice,ed., *op.cit.*, pp. 63-4.

[49] Ajeet Javed, *op.cit.*, pp. 24-5.

[50] D.S. Sharma, *Hinduism through the Ages*, (Bombay : Bharatiya Vidya Bhavan, 1973), p. 115.

joined the Sadharam Brahma Samaj which stood against all superstitious miracles and beliefs with its emphasis on reason. His indebtedness to the Samaj is revealed when Sister Nivedita quotes his words, "I also belonged to the Brahma samaj, you know, and was against all worship of images".[51] It is the rational and universalistic outlook and approach of the Samaj that prompts Vivekananada to imbibe it and made use of it in his social thought.

Another notable movement in the Vivekananda era was Arya Samaj which arose as a reaction against the influence of Islam and Christianity on the Hindu minds. It considers Vedas as the repository of knowledge about Natural Sciences, Ethics, Political duties, social laws and other subjects.[52] It maintained no fissure between social reforms and religious reforms. It assumed leadership in many movements of social reforms and worked against caste system, tried to liberate women from their social disabilities and gave an impetus to education. Its extreme deviation towards the Vedic precepts halted it from appreciating and accepting many values in Western social and political philosophies.

The Intellectual Background of Vivekananda's Teachings

The great impacts of the main incidents and messages that Vivekananda has acquired from several incidents, knowledge and wisdom from other sources that helps

---

[51]Sister Nivedita, *The Complete Works of Sister Nivedita*, (Calcutta : Ramakrishna Sarada Mission, 1968-1973),Vol.1, p. 361.

[52]Ved Prakash, *Philosophy of Dayananda* (Uttar Pradesh: Indo Vision Pvt. Ltd., 1986), p.7.

him in bringing out his ideas and ideals are discussed as the intellectual influences. The factors that laid foundation of ultimate knowledge regarding himself and the world around him are acquired definitely through the Vedantic wisdom and the resulting yearning for the actualization of divinity in man. It is the goal of the life to awaken the dormant divinity which gradually makes one acquire the virtues and qualities of strength, freedom, fearlessness and love and compassion towards the fellow beings. Vivekananda reminds us that man has the infinite spiritual resources to nourish his own personality as well as to change his socio-cultural atmosphere. Along with Vedantic influence, the *karma-sannyasa* of Bhagavad Gita and the teaching of Jesus Christ based on love and sincerity and the reason and practicality that Buddha advocates have tremendous influence on his life and thought.

Vivekananda gained knowledge of the social and economic conditions of the country whilst he undertook an extensive travel following the death of Sri Ramakrishna.[53] During these travels he met a variety of Indians from various social strata, religions and castes, princes and scholars, toilers and tillers who were reduced to poverty and wretchedness.[54] He developed sympathy for the suffering and poor people, which in turn awakened in him the universal love towards humanity

---

[53] Basant Kumar Lal, *Contemporary Indian Philosophy* (Delhi: Motilal Banarsidass, 1973), pp.1-2.
[54] Romain Rolland, *The Life of Vivekananda the Universal Gospel* (Calcutta: Advaita Asrama,1997), pp. 21-32.

which can be called "cosmic sympathy".[55] He considered the poor and the illiterates as *'Daridra Narayana'* and worked for their welfare He left India for Chicago with the name Vivekananda as suggested by Ajit Singh of Khetri which means the 'bliss of discerning wisdom'. His visit there was intended to convey the message from India and also to bring back to India not only material help but also a message based on those feature of western culture which he admired.[56] Though he was not successful in bringing money from America for eradication of the poverty of his countrymen, the effect of his bursting forth at Chicago had electrified India. It had rejuvenated India and had hastened the pace of her renaissance.

Vivekananda's address at the world parliament of religions marked a turning point as it brought about a significant change, a paradigm shift in the history of India and of the West. He had much eagerness to learn about the people of the West and the key to its economic and scientific development, while he communicated the message of Vedanta to them. His presentation on the dichotomy between Western materialism and Eastern Spirituality regaled the audience in the West. In the West, he wanted to communicate to them the message of peace, harmony of religions and equality of human beings and oneness of humanity in Vedanta. Whereas all other delegates spoke of their own faiths and creeds, Vivekananda spoke of the God of all, the essence of every faith. He declared, "The Christian is not to become a Hindu or a Buddhist, nor a Hindu or a Buddhist to become a Christian. But each must assimilate

---

[55]Makarand Paranjape, *Swami Vivekananda : Reader* (NewDelhi: Penguin Books, 2005), p.14.

[56]*The Complete Works of Swami Vivekananda*, Vol. 8, p. 322.

the spirit of the others and yet preserve their individuality and grow according to their own laws of growth".[57] He called upon to accept religious pluralism, recognizing the principle of unity in diversity in order to keep the society free from sectarianism, bigotry and fanaticism.

Vivekananda's understanding about the secrets behind the rapid materialistic development of the West has enabled him to inform and educate his countrymen on a realistic basis on how to catch up with the West in the secular sphere. He also held hopes that through these efforts he could be able to collect financial resources to help in the upliftment of the *Daridra Narayanas* among his fellow countrymen. In addition to that he wanted to familiarize himself with the social ethos, organisational, managerial techniques and methods of the West."[58] He also recognized many good things in the West that were not purely materialistic from which he believed India could and should learn. He observed that in some respects the spirit of Vedanta manifested more in the West. One such theme was the attitude of the faith in oneself which he founded exclusively in western life. He also appreciated the ability of people in the west to work together to achieve common goals. Those goals may be on the material level, but he recognized their ability to put aside differences and work together which required some degree of self-transcendence. Thus he wanted Indians to adopt the best of science, politics, social organizations and an attitude of self-confidence from the West to inspire them to live up to their own great ideals. He

---

[57] Swami Shuddhidananda, ed., *op.cit.*, p. 54.
[58] *ibid.*, p. 245.

remarks, "From my travels in various countries I have come to the conclusion that without organization nothing great and permanent can be done".[59] He wanted to apply the social ethos, organization and managerial technique and methods of the West in his own country. The social organisations and philanthropic works of the Western nations excited admiration in him. On his return to his native country he devoted himself to a life of intense public service. Although Vivekananda cites Advaitic teachings as his philosophical basis for philanthropy, scholars generally agree that his travels to the West and his contact with Christians and their religious social activism influenced his thinking considerably. Along with the teachings of Advaita Vedanta, it might be because of these interactions with the Christian missionaries that encouraged him to form the Ramakrishna Mission. A combination of Vedanta philosophy and the philanthropic ideas of the West can be considered as important contribution of Vivekananda. Thus touring the entire West, Vivekananda had a generous give and take of ideas and ideals.

After the completion of his mission, he returned to India with a chosen band of eager disciples from the West. The sight of these Western disciples in turn raised the pride of his countrymen regarding their own ancient heritage.[60] A series of lectures that he had delivered known as 'lectures from Colombo to Almora' uplifted the

---

[59] Eknath Ranade, *Swami Vivekananda's Rousing call to Hindu Nation*, (Madras: Vivekanda Kendra, 1982), p.136.

[60] S.L. Malhotra, *Social and Political Orientations of Neo-Vedanta* (NewDelhi: S.Chand and Co.,1970), p.11.

morale of the then subjugated people of Indian Society.[61] Realising that the remedy for the aforesaid condition was neither money nor education in the ordinary sense but only spiritual education he uttered, "Let man remember his true nature, divinity. Let this become a living realisation and everything else will follow – power, strength, manhood."[62] His pilgrimage to East and West opened his eyes to see the reality of the Indian social issues which made him think of an apt philosophy for the betterment of society.

Vedanta and its Influence on the Thought

Thoughts of ancient, medieval and modern periods seem to have played a prominent role in shaping his philosophy. Parallel to these Indian thoughts he was much lured by the Western social ideals. However, Vedanta the quintessence of the philosophic thought of ancient India wielded the deepest effect upon Vivekananda's thought. His lectures and writings were immensely supported by the passages from the Upanishads. The richness of this Vedantic realization accounts for the many-sidedness of his personality and message. Though he gained enormous scientific knowledge and on various fields, he kept on yearning for knowledge that was 'Real' and 'Permanent' and by which the man could be emancipated. It was the highest Vedantic knowledge of oneness which he experienced made him feel that if everything that appears to exist is essentially part of a greater reality, service towards

---

[61]R.N. Saksena, *Indian Social Thought* (Meerut: Meenakshi Prakashan, 1981), p. 163.
[62]Eastern and Western Admirers, *Reminiscences of Swami Vivekananda* (Kolkata: AdvaitaAshrama, 2004), p. 201.

others is essentially service to Brahman. There are the various social and religious aspects of his personality directly derived from the spiritual strength of Vedanta. He himself had admitted this fact in many of his lectures and writings. He had quoted in this context thus: "My teaching is my own interpretation of ancient books, in the light which my Master shed upon them. I claim no supernatural authority. Whatever is my teaching may appeal to the highest intelligence and be accepted by thinking men, the adoption of that will be my reward". [63] Thus his basic philosophy of the essential unity of everything is anchored upon the Vedanta thought of reality. In ancient and medieval thoughts there was a general indifference to ethical and social thought because of the abstractness in thought. Sankara's philosophy has to be understood as a doctrine of salvation through realisation of one's own identity with the supreme spiritual being. Though his philosophical concept had its lasting influence on further philosophical developments, but the discussion triggered off by it was mainly focused on the relation between God, man and the universe, and not at all on social questions. It was only in the nineteenth century that social relevance of the Vedantic teaching was brought out and with in this process Vivekananda played a decisive role. It was he who "brings down Vedanta to fertilize the field of common life, so that life may be raised to uncommon heights and made capable to taste Vedanta at its purest source." [64] In his paper on Hinduism, he pointed at the varied shades of the rainbow and asserted, "From the high spiritual height of the Vedanta Philosophy, of which the

---

[63] The Complete Works of Swami Vivekananda, *Vol.5*, p.186.

[64] Rajiv Mehrotra, ed., *Swami Ranganathananda: Reader* (NewDelhi: Rupa. Co, 2009), p. 377.

latest discoveries of science seem like echoes, to the low ideas of idolatry with its multifarious mythology, the agnosticism of the Buddhists, and the atheism of the Jains, each and all have a place in the Hindu religion".[65] He thus realized the all-embracing approach of Vedanta which over rides the barriers of all external and internal difference. Therefore he says that Vedanta alone can become the universal religion of man, and that no other religion is fitted for the role. It upholds a kind of metaphysical democracy by relying upon the ideal of oneness.[66] Vivekananda states that a man can look with contempt on no creature if he perceives the one spirit in all and all in the one spirit. All evils come because of relying upon differences and that all good comes from faith in equality, sameness and oneness of things.[67]

Vedanta, as any other universal religion, constitutes the essential ethical values of mankind. But Vivekananda holds that none of the Universal religions other than Vedanta had given satisfactory answers to the ethical prescriptions and proscriptions like 'why one should not injure one's neighbour and only love them instead?'The metaphysical explanation that Vedanta provides is: 'Atman is absolute and all-pervading and hence infinite. Each individual soul is a part and parcel of that universal soul which is infinite.[68] Therefore the metaphysical truth underlying all ethical codes is that in injuring his neighbour, the individual actually injures himself.

---

[65]Dushyanta Pandya, *Swami Vivekananda: The Monarch of Monks* (NewDelhi: Readworthy Publications (P) Ltd., 2009), p.161.

[66]Jawaharlal Nehru, *op.cit.*, p. 91.

[67]*The Complete Works of Swami Vivekananda*,Vol. 3, p. 194.

[68] *The Complete Works of Swami Vivekananda*, Vol. 1, p. 388.

Vivekananda had much liking for the Vedantic doctrine of non-attachment, non-covetousness and non-possessiveness. He wanted to popularise these Vedantic concepts. He said that if man lives according to the principle of non-attachment,-"with his heart to God and hands to work," [69] success or failure does not affect him. To him, "with the sense of possession comes selfishness" and under its influence man never thinks for common good and that may clear the path for other's wretchedness. Thus his social ideas based on the non-attachment and non-possessiveness finds its roots in the inspiring thoughts of Vedanta.

The metaphysical truths Vivekananda spoke of were extracted from the Vedanta philosophy, while the psychological tool employed to obtain such truth belongs to the school of Sankhya with which Advaita philosophy had severe doctrinal differences.[70] He regarded both the systems as rational and scientific in its approach.[71] Vivekananda had addressed Sage Kapila, the proponent of Sankya philosophy as the greatest psychologist the world has ever known.[72] Speaking from his position Vivekananda was forced to admit Vedanta's indebtedness to Sankhya thought. It is with the support of the Samkhya theory of gunas he explains the classification of human personality. The qualities of sattva (luminous), rajas (passionate) and tamas (darkness) are inherent in every being. Men differ in accordance with the

---

[69] *ibid.*, p.12 .

[70] Amiya.P.Sen, *The Indispensable Vivekananda: An Anthology of Our Times* (New Delhi: Permanent Black, 2006), p. 40.

[71] *The Complete Works of Swami Vivekananda*, Vol.2, p. 445.

[72] *The Complete Works of Swami Vivekananda*, Vol.3, p.42.

predominance of one or the other of these qualities. Accordingly it is these qualities which make one person a teacher, another, an administrator, a business man or a worker .What is intended here is that each person is responsible for what he is. Man can improve and integrate his personality as these qualities do not remain fixed. Thus in the analysis of human nature with its different temperaments and capacities, Vivekananda's thought finds its indebtedness to the psycho-physical aspect of man explored in the Samkya thought.

Impact of Bhagavad Gita on the Philosophy of Vivekananda

The impact of Bhagavad Gita on Vivekananda was tremendous, for it is a poem of crisis, of political and social crisis and of crisis in the spirit of man. It deals with the individual's duty and social behaviour, of the application of ethics to human life and of the spiritual outlook that should govern all. In the Gita, an action for social betterment and social service, altruistic and humanitarian action are recommended, but these actions must be done in a spirit of detachment and not concerned with its results.[73] Vivekananda holds the Gita as a practical and the simplified version of the theoretical teachings of the sameness and omnipresence of the supreme soul preached in the Vedanta. In a lecture delivered in San Fransisco in 1900, he asserted the Gita as the commentary on the Upanishad[74]. It is in consonance with the teachings of the Gita, Vivekananda states that the man who sees the Supreme Lord dwelling alike in

---

[73] *The Complete Works of Swami Vivekananda*, Vol.7, p.19.

[74] *The Complete Works of Swami Vivekananda*, Vol. 1, p. 446.

all beings, the imperishable in things that perish can do service to others selflessly[75]. God is in us and we have only to turn within to realise the truth. The removal of ignorance is the only solution to all evil. It is the thoughtless man dives into deep lakes, penetrates into jungles, ascends steep hills in search of flowers for the worship of God while the one lotus which he can offer, is his own mind.[76] He who is ignorant of the Lord dwelling in every one's mind cannot serve others selflessly. Thus the wonderful idea in the Vedanta, of the sameness and omnipresence of the supreme soul has been preached in the Gita also for the elevation of the human race.

Though a follower of the path of renunciation, it was counter balanced by Vivekananda's real concern for social development. In that sense he was a true *karmayogin* practicing detachment and not abstaining from life and action.[77] Thus *karmayoga* according to him is not only to be practiced in individual life, it is to be sincerely practiced in social level also. He quoted frequently and copiously from the verses of the Gita for the purpose of dispelling India's social degeneration and inertia through its vibrant message of activism. He owed much to the Gita for its doctrine of 'work for work's sake', renunciation and service, modes of worship, resistance to injustice and tyranny. Being a firm believer of karmayoga which has been elaborately

---

[75] *The Complete Works of SwamiVivekananda*, Vol. 3, pp. 193-4

[76] Robert A.McDermott, *The Basic writings of S. Radhakrishnan* (Mumbai: Jaico Publishing House, 2007), p.55.

[77] Diane Collison and Robert Wilkinson, *op.cit.*, p.81.

dealt with in the second and third chapter of the Gita, he has stated that intense activity is a necessity for every man.[78]

Vivekananda laid greater stress on the Gita ideal of cultivation of a detached mind. He realised that mere physical help cannot alleviate all the miseries of the world; it can never bring about permanent satisfaction. Man's needs and miseries will find no end until his nature changes. As long as man is in the embodied state, he cannot escape from action. Quoting the Gita, Vivekananda said, "Thinking of objects arose attachment to them from attachment longing and from longing anger grows.[79] The disciplines of the senses is the sum total of the means of attaining spiritual enrichment. The self-controlled person is tainted neither by sin nor by other evils. Control of senses and the control of mind and thereby giving up all desires for enjoyment in earth or heaven is needed to man to know his own real nature. As he further said, "The less the sense enjoyment, the higher the life of man".[80] The Gita speaks on the necessity of celibacy and keeping away from lust, if one wanted to attain real piety. He holds that "being a slave of lust is just animal existence."[81] He said, "We may convert every house in the country into a charity asylum, we may fill the land with hospitals, but the misery of man will still continue to exist until man's character changes".[82] Individual miseries grow with the multiplication of wants. "If

---

[78] *The Complete Works of Swami Vivekananda*, Vol.1, p.34.

[79] *The Complete Works of SwamiVivekananda*, Vol.4, p. 410.

[80] *ibid.*, p. 13.

[81] Dushyanta Pandya, *op.cit.*, p. 227.

[82] *The Complete Works of SwamiVivekananda*, Vol.1, p. 53.

the power to satisfy our desire is increased in arithmetic progression, the power of desire is increased in geometric progression",[83] he had once said. He believes that karma without attachment is the only passport to human happiness that can mitigate his misery and suffering.

Quoting the Gita, Vivekananda said "To work you have the right, but not to the fruit thereof"[84] It enjoins that *Karma* is not so much the abandonment of action, but it is the performance of action in the spirit of *Sannyasa* or renunciation.[85] Inaction is condemned and action must be in accordance with the highest ideal.[86] Here *sannyasa* or the spirit of *Vairagya* is a quality of mind that frees man from hatred and desire. In consonance with this purpose in the Gita, he asked everyone to work only for its own sake with one's mind free from egoism, desire and fear. The inspiring motto of the Ramakrishna movement 'for the freedom of oneself and for the welfare of the world' which Vivekananda coined had its origin from the socio-spiritualistic approach in the Karma-Yoga. The continuous attempt that is seen in the Gita which harmonises social activity with spiritual adventure had its effect on Vivekananda's life and thought.

Through narrating the story of the *Vyadha* in the Gita, Vivekananda establishes that an ideal man is realized not in one who abandons social living and leading a life

---

[83] *The Complete Works of SwamiVivekananda*, Vol. 4, p. 172

[84] *The Complete Works of SwamiVivekananda*, Vol.4 p. 159.

[85] *Eastern and Western Admirers, op.cit.*, p. 281.

[86] *The Complete Works of SwamiVivekananda*, Vol. 7, p. 32.

of a renunciate in forests and caves, but it may also be equally realised by dutiful men living in each and every condition of life. The message conveyed in it is that a spiritual aspirant need not give up the company of women or any householders, but can live in the world and can work for the welfare of the world with a right frame of mind[87]. Giving support to Gita's inclination to duties, Vivekananda asserts that each and every man can realize the truth by doing duties depending upon one's condition and position in life. In order to achieve the highest aim, he alludes everyone to do his work in conformity with the ideals and activities of the society in which he is born[88]. Certain ideals and activities do not prevail in all societies and countries. The nature of one's duties will change in accordance with the environment. Hence no man, asserted Vivekananda, is to be judged by the mere nature of his duties, but each man should be judged by the manner and spirit in which they perform them.

Buddha's Teachings and Its Influence

In his lectures and discourses, Vivekananda had beautifully expressed his conviction that modern India requires assimilating the great intellect of Sankara and the great heart of Buddha. He depicted the Buddha as the fulfillment of the spiritual thought of the Upanisads which had preceded him. It is by the Buddha the moral side of the philosophy of the Vedanta was laid stress upon because he set in motion the highest Vedanta metaphysics, by avoiding the two extremes of the pursuit of worldly

---

[87] *The Complete Works of Swami Vivekananda*, Vol. 7, p. 32.

[88] *The Complete Works of Swami Vivekananda*, Vol. 1, p. 64.

desires and severe ascetic discipline culminating in the annihilation of body.[89] Vivekananda also seems in line with him while he adopts a moderate position throughout his thought. Both were real embodiments of the Vedanta practicalised. The teachings of the Buddha shares some point of similarity with that of Vivekananda.

What Vivekananda admires so much in Buddha is his a strong brain and a clear mind free of nonsensical ideas. As he refers to the saying of the Buddha against the superstitious tradition, he elucidates: Buddha said, "These ceremonials are all wrong. There is but one ideal in the world. Destroy all delusions; what is true will remain…work not for any superstition, not to please any God, not to get any reward…"[90] Vivekananda observed that the Buddha was the first who dared to say "Believe not because some old manuscripts are produced, believe not because it is your national belief, because you have been made to believe it from your childhood, but reason it all out and after you have analysed it, then if you find that it will do good to one and all, believe it, live up to it."[91] Vivekananada, like Buddha was also not satisfied with the secondhand evidence to believe in miracles and marvels which cannot be empirically known. Both of them agreed with the faith they inherited on the fundamentals of metaphysics and ethics, but protested against certain practices which were in vogue at their time.

---

[89] *The Complete Works of SwamiVivekananda*, Vol. 2, p. 495.

[90] Mohit Chakraborty, *Swami Vivekananda: Visionary of Truth* (Delhi : Abhijeet Publications, 2010), p.114.

[91] Swami Vivekananda, *Karma Yoga* (Kolkata: AdvaitaAshrama, 2009), p.131.

Vivekananda was much inspired by the Buddha's message of universal love and benevolence for all. Buddha's message to overcome anger by kindness, evil by good[92] had tremendous impact on him. The spread of the religion of Buddha in India despite its denial of God and soul is simply because of its stress on marvelous love which overflowed a large heart and devoted itself to the service not only of all men but of all living things, a love which did not care for anything except to find a way of release from suffering for all beings. His love was not only towards human but extended to animal kingdom also. He was the first in the world to stand as champion of the dumb animals. By criticizing animal sacrifice as superstition, Buddha said, "If sacrificing an animal is good, sacrificing a man is better".[93] And in order to prevent such sacrifices he was even willing to offer himself instead of an animal's life. The Buddha's advice to abandon the feeling of pride and superiority in matters of faith had great impact on Vivekananda. Non-egoism is the need of both individuals and nations. Sharing this view Vivekananda said that it is impossible to get spiritual development without considering oneself as the lowest of the low.[94] Everyone should learn to look upon the whole world as one's own, as there is nothing strange and alien in this world. Buddha was the first to break down the caste, standing between man

---

[92]Jawaharlal Nehru, *op.cit.,* p. 128.

[93]Swami Adiswarananda, ed., *Vivekananda: World Teacher* (NewDelhi: Rupa Publications India Pvt. Ltd., 2007), p.141.

[94]Eastern and Western Admirers, *op.cit.*, p. 322.

and man.⁹⁵ Thus not only the quality of tremendous love towards all beings, but also the boldness and the fearlessness that the Buddha showed while dealing with certain superstitions and beliefs made Vivekananda an innate lover of him.⁹⁶ Through the epithets addressed on the Buddha like 'Thou the breaker of caste, destroyer of privilege and preacher of equality of all beings,' Vivekananda tried to disclose the social egalitarianism in his thought.

Vivekananda was much influenced by the Buddhist ideal of Bodhisattva in envisaging his idea of mass-liberation.⁹⁷ The ethical path that the Buddha insisted is the path of service, to help others to become holy. For the bodhisattva the goal was not nirvana but the experiential awareness of the ultimate reality, which is one with compassion.⁹⁸ The bodhisattva strove to be of service to other rather than attain final release. Buddhists declare that each individual has in him a spark of the Divine and could become a bodhisattva person who strove to be of service to others rather than attain final release. When Vivekananda presented himself before his Master, after receiving the highest non-dual experience, the unity of all existence, he commanded his disciple to follow the most sublime ideal and mission of a bodhisattva. ⁹⁹ He viewed the Buddha as a person who had commissioned for the work of liberating all

---

⁹⁵Marie Louise Burke, *Swami Vivekananda in the West: New Discoveries* (Kolkata : AdvaitaAshrama, 1994), vol. 2, p. 275.

⁹⁶ *The Complete Works of SwamiVivekananda*, Vol. 8, p. 103.

⁹⁷BasantKumarlal, *op.cit.,* p.2

⁹⁸ *President Radhakrishnan's Speeches and Writings* (New Delhi: Director , Publication Division, Patalia House, 1969), p. 326

⁹⁹Swami Suddhidananda, ed.,*op.cit.*, p.422.

from the miseries of the world. In recent times also Gandhiji and S. Radhakrishnan uphold the sarvamukti ideal rather than seeking one's own liberation. It might also be the influence of the Buddistic saying *'Bahujanahitaya Bahujanasukhaya'* that prompted Vivekananda to thunder that by seeking one's own salvation, one will go to hell. It is the salvation of others that one must seek and even if he has to go to hell in working for others, that is worth more than to gain heaven by seeking one's own salvation.[100] Thus he appraised the Buddha as a humanist interested in the perennial problems of man.

Even though the Buddha does not depend upon God, observed Vivekananda, his religion is directed to evolve a God out of man which forms the great truth in every religion.[101] Perfection not only comes from belief or faith alone but from the disinterested performance of action. Vivekananda looked upon the Buddha as a 'God man' and the ideal *KarmaYogin*.[102] Unlike many others, the Buddha's search for truth is not intended for any metaphysical inquisitiveness but for the alleviation of misery of others. Vivekananda also held a similar position while stating that it is through the heart that the Lord can be seen and not through the intellect. The intellect is only the street cleaner, cleansing the path for us, a secondary worker, the police man, but the policeman is not a positive necessity for the workings of society. He is only to stop disturbances to check wrong doing and that is all the work required for the

---

[100] His Eastern and Western Disciples, *op.cit.*, Vol. 2, p. 426.
[101] *The Complete Works of Swami Vivekananda*, Vol.1, p. 19
[102] Rekha Jhanji, *The Philosophy of Vivekananda* (New Delhi: Aryan Books International, 2007), p.151.

intellect."[103] Hence the relevance of his teachings lies in its social and political realms rather than its doctrines.

Vivekananda had some aversion towards the Buddha's decision regarding the use of *Pali* language instead of Sanskrit. He said: "Even the great Buddha made one false step when he stopped the Sanskrit language from being studied by the masses."[104] He gave immense importance to the use of Sanskrit language. In his view, the teachings of Ramananda, Kabir and Chaitanya failed to survive long because of their inability to promote Sanskrit language.[105] Sir William Jones observed that the Sanskrit language as more perfect and refined than the Greek and the Latin and yet have a stronger affinity to both languages.[106] William Jones was followed by scholars like Max Muller, Charles Wilkins and others who mastered Sanskrit along with many ancient languages of India. They translated many works in classical Sanskrit and other modern Indian languages into European languages. Their interpretation of the Vedas and other Indian scriptures help to kindle a national pride and nationalistic feeling in the minds of educated Indians. Vivekananda opined that the Sanskrit language which was the monopoly of people belonging to higher classes have to be provided to all irrespective of castes, then only their raising be possible.[107]

---

[103]Swami Vivekananda, *Practical Vedanta* (Kolkata : Advaita Ashrama, 2007), pp. 28-29.

[104]*The Complete Works of Swami Vivekananda*, Vol.3, p. 291.

[105]*ibid.*, p. 290-1.

[106]Jawaharlal Nehru, *op.cit.*, p. 165.

[107]*The Complete Works of Swami Vivekananda*, Vol.3, p. 291

Not mere acquisition of knowledge but learning Sanskrit is the one way he recommended to become cultured.[108] He criticized the Buddha for promoting *Pali*, a language accessible to all instead of Sanskrit. But no one can deny the fact that the Buddha's teachings made the spread of knowledge far and wide and could make a revolution by rapid and immediate results. The dislike Vivekananda expressed to this type of an approach definitely stands for criticism. The Buddha's vision making worship available to all through vernacular is being accepted the world over in our times. This in fact point to the prophetic vision of the Buddha.

Influence of Jesus Christ in the Teachings of Vivekananda

Along with Indian influences, Vivekananda was open to accept the ideals of Christianity. He used to carry the 'Imitation of Christ' and the *Bhagavad Gita* with him wherever he went[109]. He had also translated the same book into Bengali to spread the spirit of humility and self-renunciation as practised by Christ, among the Bengalis.[110] From a lecture delivered in Los Angels, his appreciation for Christ can be traced: "...there are giants who embody, as it were, almost the whole of the past and stretch out their hands over future also. They are the sign pots here and there, directing the march on humanity; they are verily giants, their shadows covering the

---

[108]*Idem.*

[109]Romain Rolland, *The Life of Vivekananda and the Universal Gospel* (Calcutta: Advaita Ashrama, 1997), p. 23.

[110]*The Complete Works of Swami Vivekananda*, Vol. 8, p. 159.

earth; they stand undying, eternal."[111] He was immensely impressed by the strength of character – the soul force that the 'man of the cross' possessed[112]. He felt that it required a supreme spiritual strength to forgive the oppressor even while suffering from acute physical torture. He accepted Christ as a perfect embodiment of spiritual values and considered that knowledge of his life would benefit any culture.[113] He espoused the ideal of service and love from Christianity. He had great admiration for the Gospel of Jesus which has its insistence on every true believer to renounce greed and not social life in toto. Blind love for wealth and material pleasure would be avoided to attain spiritual perfection. The Bible says: "It is easier for a camel to get though a needle's eye than for a rich man to get into the kingdom of God."[114] Vivekananda was highly motivated by Christ's self-renunciation which he incorporated the in the Hindu traditional ideal of renunciation of the world.

Vivekananda made an analysis of Vedanta and Christian conception of God and adroitly blended Christian view of God with that of Vedanta's divinity of the soul which is also helpful in solving the problems of religious intolerance and racism. Man contains within him the spark of divinity and his hopeful faith in the possibility of man's redemption contains elements that profoundly resemble the Christian notion

---

[111] Swami Adiswarananda, *Vivekananda World Teacher : His Teachings on Spiritual Unity of Mankind* (NewDelhi: Rupa Publications India Pvt. Ltd.,2007), p. 122.

[112] Basant Kumar Lal, *op.cit.*, p.3.

[113] Marie Louise Burke, *op.cit.*, p. 202.

[114] Sivaramakrishna and SumitaRoy,ed., Perspectives on Ramakrishna-Vivekananda Vedanta Tradition pp. 205-206., Mathew 19:24

of the kingdom of God within man.[115] Vivekananda states that only when a man has developed a high state of spirituality he can understand that the kingdom of Heaven is within him.[116] "Think not that you are trampled upon and tyrannized over, as if you were slaves, for within you is something that can never be tyrannized over, never be trampled upon, never be troubled, and never be killed. You are all sons of God, immortal spirit."[117]

Vivekananda condemned the concept of original sin in Christianity perhaps of his affinity towards the Vedantic idea of the innate goodness of soul.[118] He considered the story of Adam and Eve not as a point of historical fact but as a mythological representation of man's relationship with God. It is the responsibility of man to choose to order his whole being in correspondence with God or not.[119] Here man's degeneration is the consequence of his own ignorant use of free will. Myths are often passed off as religious history, and symbols are apprehended as the real thing rather than what they represent. Miraculous births and supernatural happenings are not the monopoly of any particular religion, but are common to the myths of all religions.[120] Hence Vivekananda showed that there is no need to treat myths as historical facts.

---

[115] *The Complete Works of Swami Vivekananda*, Vol. I, p. 324.

[116] Basant Kumar Lal, *op.cit.*, p. 3.

[117] Swami Vivekananda, *Christ the messanger* (Kolkata : AdvaitaAshrama), p. 21.

[118] *The Complete Works of Swami Vivekananda* Vol. I, p.11.

[119] GautamSen, *The Mind of Swami Vivekananda* (Mumbai: Jaico Publishing House, 2011), p. 43.

[120] *ibid.*, p. XV.

Vivekananda is unique in that he is neither in thrall to the thoughts of the past nor is he willing to discard everything from it. It was these multiple influences of thoughts which originate not only in India, but in every other country and in every other period of civilization that widen his vision and thought to a universal one. He felt that humanity is in need of spiritual awakening to conquer materialism and its miseries. He was influenced by the thoughts of the East and that of the West, thoughts of the modern as well as that of the past periods. Any individual human being or race or nation must necessarily have certain roots in the past which is the accumulation of generations of experience and wisdom. A tree cannot sustain in roots alone. As it will wither, unless it is placed out in the open, in the sun and the free air. Likewise a person can develop only through an acquisition of an open mind. Without dynamic outlook, there may be stagnation and decay and devoid of some fixed basic principle there is likely to be disintegration and destruction. In short, in his thoughts and social service, he was driven by his feelings of his passionate devotion to his master Sri Ramakrishna, by his heartfelt awareness of human suffering and poverty that acquired through his experience as a wandering monk, by his earnest conviction implanted in him by his success in the West that the India and the West needed each other. His larger and multiple influences made himself feels as a citizen of the world-community. An analysis on Vivekananda's life and thought reveals that it is stemmed on a fixed foundation of ancient Indian scriptures and at the same time it also has a dynamic modern outlook because of its exposure to the thoughts of the West.

CHAPTER III

THE METAPHYSICAL PERSPECTIVES OF VIVEKANANDA

The material of Vivekananda's social ideas including his cultural rejuvenation, social modernization and progressive reformation all have a strong metaphysical footing. But it was not his own personal innovation as it belongs to the thought inherent in the depths of Indian spiritual lore. Most of the ideas in his Neo-Vedanta are derived from the Vedanta, the Bhagavad Gita, the Yoga philosophy and also from the teachings of Sri Ramakrishna Paramahamsa.[1] The outline of this new Vedanta has been drawn from the thoughts of Sri Ramakrishna, but it was presented in more clear, consistent and convincing manner by his disciple. In this context Mr. Satischandra Chatterjee remarks thus, "...Swami Vivekananda is a commentary on Sri Ramakrishna. But the commentator with his gaint intellect and profound understanding made such distinctive contributions that his commentary becomes itself a philosophy, just as Sankara's commentary on the Vedanta-Sutra is by itself a philosophy".[2]

---

[1] A.V. Ratna Reddy, *Political Philosophy of Swami Vivekananda*, (New Delhi: Sterling Publishers Pvt. Ltd., 1984), p.1.

[2] Shail Kumari Singh, *Religious and Moral Philosophy of Swami Vivekananda*, (New Delhi: Janaki Prakashan, 1983), p.143.

As mentioned in the previous chapter, the social authoritarianism and religious orthodoxy that prevailed in India urged Vivekananda to expand the areas of Vedantic thought to social and political issues of his days. A self sufficient social philosophy must also have its own metaphysical presupposition. Dr. S. Radhakrishnan has said that any ethical and social theory must be grounded in metaphysics.[3] Any system of knowledge if built entirely upon sense perception will never last. The grouping of facts or generalization is not possible without some abstract notion as the background.[4] Thus his conception regarding man and society is deeply rooted in the Vedantic metaphysics. He determined to provide the thought with a practicality and forcefulness that the subject desperately needed at that time.

Reconciliation of Advaita, Visistadvaita and Dvaita Thoughts

Vivekananda's neo-Vedantic structure accommodates the three different paths of dualism, qualified non dualism and Advaitism and various shades in between, as the stages of growth to reach the same God. Though he was more inclined towards monism, he had no repugnance towards qualified monism and dualism[5]. Like the traditional thinkers he did not put Dvaitism against Advaitism, but following his Guru, he upholds all systems as different stages of growth on the way to realize divine

---

[3] P.J.Saher, *Eastern Wisdom and Western Thought* (London: George Allen and Union Ltd, 1969),p.113.

[4] Swami Vivekananda, *The Complete works of Swami Vivekananda* (Calcutta: Advaita Ashrama, 2003), Vol .4, p.377.

[5] R.N.Sharma, *Contemporary Indian Philosophy* (New Delhi: Atlantic Publishers and Distributors, 1991), p.96.

power in the human self. Considering every thought other than Advaita as an imperfect expression of truth, he says, "A higher truth does not negate a lower truth, but only perfects it."[6] Thus an ascend to the summit of Advaita was through the bottom rungs of Dvaita and Visistadvaita[7]. It is from truth and not from untruth that one proceeds to further truth. Thus a gradual progress is suggested and an evolutionary process in which seeking of truth passes from lower stages to the ultimate stage of Advaita. Another reason for his acceptance of diverse paths is because of his attitude that, diversity of religion is the plan of nature. All religions having the same saving power; one can choose any religion according to one's abilities and temperament. He said "A man must follow the tendencies peculiar to himself... but if we try to force him into another path, he will lose what he has already attained and will become worthless... One religion cannot suit all."[8] This seems a healthy solution for maintaining social harmony.

The kind of philosophy he advocates has a universal outlook, unifying thoughts of varying places and races with its inherent vision of universal selfhood. Being based on the unity and universality he tried to reconcile different shades of thoughts in his philosophy. The more we believe in the oneness of life, the less we remain confined in a particular thought rejecting all the others. This is much disclosed

---

[6] Thomas Manummel .S.J, *The Advaita of Vivekananda* (Madras: J.R. Publications Pvt. Ltd.,1991), p.102.

[7] *The Complete Works of Swami Vivekananda*,Vol.3, p.324.

[8] *ibid.*, p.358.

in Vivekananda's universal acceptance of all thoughts. He realized that a human philosophy can neither dualistic alone nor can it be non dualistic alone. It perceives the relation between the dream and the dreamer, the Real and the unreal, the consciousness and the thought. While accepting Advaita, he refuses to stop with it; he accepts duality, but refuses to remain limited to it. For him, Dvaita, Visishtadvaita and Advaita are just three phases in the development of the soul which reaches the highest goal with the perfection of Oneness. Such Oneness however is not against the dualistic or Dvaita concept but nullifies it by identifying unity in diversity and by visualizing God, Self and the Universe as one. The teaching that envisages no ultimate difference between man and man, promotes to foster a humanistic and peaceful social living. By trying to bring into harmony that which forever is and that which is bound by time and space, it becomes a truly human philosophy of truth. It links humans with humans, humans with nature and humans with God.

Vivekananda postulated that social activities act in a Dvaita and Visistadvaitic stages are steps to the Advaitic stage of complete perfection. Without realizing complete perfection one cannot exercise utter unselfishness as a divine free will at the lower stages.[9] If one does social activity at the semi perfect stage, one will be attached to the result of the action which leads to *karma* and rebirth. There is no guarantee that the unselfish motivation of the divine nature is always present in all our activities at the lower stages to make sure that we are perfectly free from Karmic law. In reality,

---

[9] Abraham Stephen, *The Social Philosophy of Vivekananda: Its Relevance to Modern India* (Delhi: ISPCK, 2005), p.257.

Vivekananda accepts the view that perfection as utter unselfishness which can be attainable only in the Advaitic stage.[10] He also upholds that gradual perfection must be obtained by unselfish social service. In the light of these arguments it can be concluded that without realizing Oneness at the Advaitic stage one cannot perform unselfish service to the society as Vivekananda pointed out. All our works in other stages, dualism and qualified non-dualism are attached to selfish motives which bind one to rebirth. Therefore attaining perfection by self-denying social service is not possible unless the man attains the Advaitic position of Oneness.

Concept of Brahman

In accordance with the Advaitic concept, Brahman is conceived as the sole reality. Vivekananda distinguishes between Brahman in itself and Brahman in the Universe. But the indeterminate and the determinate are not exclusive. The two are like two sides of one reality. Regarding indeterminate Absolute (*Para Brahman*) he is of the opinion that all attempts of language, calling Him father, or brother or our dearest friend are attempts of objectification which is impossible[11]. He is the eternal subject of everything, so '*Neti Neti*' (not this, not this) is all that can be said of Brahman[12]. In expressing some ideas of the Absolute, we thereby restrict it so that it ceases to be the Absolute. Anything that is expressed by reason has its limits. In this

---

[10] *The Complete Works of Swami Vivekananda*, Vol.1, pp.399-0.

[11] *The Complete Works of Swami Vivekananda*, Vol.2, p.134.

[12] S.Radhakrishnan, *History of Philosophy: Eastern and Western* (London: George Allen and Unwin Ltd., 1957), p.225.

sense a God known, is no more God. Vivekananda tried to disclose the fact that it is impossible to know Brahman by reason. Only by merging with the Brahman and thereby freeing oneself from the fetters of the material world, the knowledge of Brahman can be attained. Knowledge of any thing means the limitation of the thing known. Brahman is unlimited and infinite. Infinite cannot be two, but one. If there exist two realities says Vivekananda, then one will limit the other and both become finite. Brahman by definition is infinite and hence He is one. Here also Vivekananda does not deviate from the traditional Vedanta view of Nirguna Brahman. Thinking of Brahman in negative characters, asserts Vivekananda does not point out, it as a non entity. While it is non empirical, it is also inclusive of the whole empirical world. Besides the negative characterization, positive qualities are also used to affirm the positivity of being.

As no enquiry into its nature can be instituted without some description, *Sat-Chit-Ananda* (Existence-knowledge-Bliss) is the highest concept of God possible to the mind[13]. When one is describing Brahman as *'Sacchidananda'*, he is only indicating the shores of an indescribable beyond. Vivekananda considers *'Sacchidananda'*, as only an approximate definition and *Neti Neti* as the essential definition[14], which is in contrast with S.Radhakrishnan's view of *Sacchidananda* as

---

[13] *The Complete Works of Swami Vivekananda*,Vol.I, p.334.

[14] *The Complete Works of Swami Vivekananda*, Vol.8, p.362.

the essential definition. Brahman is neither known nor unknown but something infinitely higher than either. [15]

Vivekananda's explanation of *Sacchidananda* in terms of rational criteria is as follows: The first principle of reasoning is that the particular is explained by the general, the general by the more general until we come to the universal. He states the 'existence' as the most universal concept.[16] All and everything comes under the one concept of existence. The very nature of reality namely Atman or Brahman is nothing but existence. Brahman is the last generalization to which one can arrive.

Again, he speaks about something new that is not found in the Advaita Vedanta viz., Brahman is *ananda*, i.e., bliss, which is the same as love.[17] The concept of love is absolutely alien to the very spirit of the Advaita philosophy. Here one might wonders if Vivekananda shares the Christian concept of Love which is the essence of the Trinitarian unity. However this seems to be a remote possibility as revealed in his statement: "But no sooner is the essence of *chit* realized, than the essence of *Ananda* is also realized. Because what is *chit* is, verily, the same as *Ananda*".[18] Thus, though we know the Absolute, in three apparently different attributes, they are not different, but one reality. In reply to the Samkhya criticism that the one and the same thing cannot have three essences, it is pointed out by the

---

[15] *The Complete Works of Swami Vivekananda*, Vol.2, p.133.

[16] *The Complete Works of Swami Vivekananda*, Vol.1, p.370.

[17] Dr.RomaChaudhari, *Vivekananda : The Great Spiritual Teacher* (Kolkata : Advaita Ashrama, 2008), p. 283.

[18] *ibid.*, p.283.

Vedantists that *Sat, Chit* and *Ananda* are by no means, three different essences rather they are the three aspects of the very same essence.[19] Through the approximate definition of Brahman as *Sachchidananda*, Vivekananda asserts that everyone from the highest angle to the lowest particle of matter is definitely the little expressions of the Existence-knowledge-Bliss.

Concept of World

As against the traditional Vedantism, that this world to be unreal or illusory, Vivekananda speaks so openly and definitely in defence of the reality of this world. Religions of the world also hold a similar view that this world is nothing, and beyond this world is something which is very real. If the world were altogether unreal, we could not progress from unreal to real. Vivekananda asked that if this world is a means towards attaining the next, how this world can be nothing.[20] If a passage is possible from the empirical to the Real, the Real is to be found in the empirical also, so the world is real as based on Brahman, it is unreal by itself.

This metaphysical fissure between Brahman and the Universe is explained through the view of apparent creation or *Vivarthavada*.[21] Brahman is viewed as the cause of the Universe; it becomes relative, transient, finite and having form, when seen in the objects and phenomena of nature. The highest expression must have been

---

[19] Makarand Paranjape, *SwamiVivekananda: A Contemporary Reader* (NewDelhi: Penguin Books, 2005), p.457.

[20] *The Complete Works of Swami Vivekananda*, Vol.8, p.4.

[21] *The Complete Works of Swami Vivekananda*, Vol.1, p.363.

there in the germ state in minute form and this whole world is the involution of that cosmic life which is everywhere. To make it clearer Vivekananda tells that everything that one sees, feels or hears is His projection.[22] In other words it can also be said that the world is 'the Lord Himself' and He is both the efficient and the material cause of this universe.

Vivekananda has attempted to explain the question of how the emanation takes place while the Brahman remains ever complete and undiminished ?[23] The answer which he provides to this difficulty is the *Vivarthavada* version. Along with Advaitins, Vivekananda considers the whole Universe to be an apparent evolution of the Absolute. The Absolute is not really, but apparently the material cause of the universe. In *Vivartha vada* or Appearance theory, there is no actual transformation of Brahman into the differentiated world.[24] The world of duality is suggested to be seeming. The existence of duality is not admitted to be absolutely real. It is not like the transformation of milk into curd. The appearance of Brahman to relative consciousness as the differentiated world is like the appearance of a straight stick as a bent one, when it is immersed in a bowl of water.

Conception Regarding Maya

Again Vivekananda points out that the time, space and causation (*desa- kala-nimitta*) is responsible for the apparent differentiation that we perceive in the world.

---

[22] *ibid.*, p.362.

[23] *The Complete Works of Swami Vivekananda,* Vol.2, p.363.

[24] *ibid.*, p.130.

The Absolute cannot descend to the level of the world without passing through time, space and causation. This is a very bold idea of Advaita according to Vivekananda[25]. But he did not consider space, time and causality as separate, independent and isolated essences existing outside objects and phenomena of the material world. We cannot see anything outside the space, yet we do not know space. We cannot perceive anything outside of time yet we do not know time. We cannot understand anything except in terms of causality, yet we do not know what causation is. Time, space and causality are in and through every phenomenon, but they are not phenomena. They are the cause of multiplicity.[26] The sum total of this space, time and causation is what Vivekananda calls Maya.

Vivekananda's views regarding Maya are fundamentally in agreement with that of Sankara who speaks of Maya as the magical power of the Absolute which makes His Oneness manifold. He had delivered four lectures in London to explain the theory of Maya, its origin and its meaning. He argues that the oldest idea of Maya that is inscribed in Vedic literature has its meaning as delusion.[27] A long time after the Rig Vedic period the word 'maya' is spoken of as a mist covering the Reality.[28] Vivekananda does not support the commonly used meaning of Maya as illusion. The word Maya does not mean that the world is pure illusion, but our world is full of contradictions and to that extent it can be regarded as unreal. He says Maya is said to

---

[25] *idem.*

[26] *The Complete Works of Swami Vivekananda*, Vol.2, p. 136.

[27] *ibid.,* p.88.

[28] *idem.*

be seeing the real as something else and not as it is.[29] He asserts that Maya is what makes the difference between one man and another, between all animals and man, and between gods and men.[30] It is because of the influence of Maya the unreal is taken for the real. In this connection Vivekananda takes up the classical illustration of rope-snake illusion by stating the apparent presentation of snake on a rope until the delusion vanishes. Similar is the case with regard to the Universe. Using Kant's terminology, Vivekananda explains that Maya is phenomenon, the substance is noumenon. "There is the real 'me' which nothing can destroy, and there is the phenomenal 'me' which is continually changing and disappearing."[31] Everything that exists has two aspects. One is noumenal, unchanging and indestructible and the other is phenomenal, changing and destructible. He also speaks of other exemplars in which the difference in the mental state of the onlooker can make the same subject appear differently. He avers: In the darkness of night, a stump of a tree is looked upon as a ghost by some persons, as a police station by a robber, as a friend by someone waiting for his companion.[32] In all these instances the stump of the tree does not change, but the imitations are all in the minds of those who see it.

Everything in the sense world affirms Vivekananda is dependent and interdependent, relative and correlative. These are distinguishable from the ultimate

---

[29] *The Complete Works of Swami Vivekananda*, Vol.8, p.26.

[30] Swami Vivekanada, *Advaita Vedanta: The Scientific Religion* (Kolkata: Advaita Ashrama, 2005), p.43.

[31] *The Complete Works of Swami Vivekananda*, Vol.8, p. 247.

[32] *The Complete Works of Swami Vivekananda*, Vol.1, p. 418.

Reality only through name and form. Any object of nature is substance plus name and form. This form and name are not immutable or indestructible, but the substance remains the same.[33] All the differentiation in substance is made by name and form. So long as one perceives the differences they are real. Thus Vivekananda agrees with Sankara when he says "Maya is neither absolute zero nor non existence".[34] It is defined neither as existence nor as non existence. Maya is not existence because it can be said only of the Absolute. Again it cannot be said that it is non existence, because if it were nonexistent, it could never produce the phenomenon. He illustrates this with the help of another analogy of ocean and waves. He says: The waves are the same as the ocean and yet they are different. We cannot think wave form as something separate from the ocean and yet the wave is not the same as the ocean. Even though the form vanishes when the wave subsides, the form was not a delusion as we perceive it for some time. Similarly Maya cannot be defined as non existence any more than it can be define as existence.[35] It is an intermediate form between the absolute being and the non- being. It can be defined only by the word 'relativity' that science has deal with.

The western critics have raised criticism that if the foundational truth is Atman-Brahman, then there is no scope for removal of the suffering of the downtrodden and the exploited because they are already identical with Brahman.

---

[33] *The Complete Works of Swami Vivekananda*, Vol.8, p.247.

[34] *The Complete Works of Swami Vivekananda*, Vol.1, pp.363-4.

[35] Romain Rolland, *The World Religious of Vivekananda* (Delhi: Vijaya Goel, 2005), pp.24-5.

They are already perfect and do not have any isolated existence. Besides since the world is maya or illusion, there is no relevance in saying that we can improve the nature of the world by act of charity. But Vivekananda gave a new dimension to the concept of Maya and has distinctly explained how and why this can be done. According to Vivekananda, maya does not mean illusion. The maya of the Vedanta in its developed form is neither idealism nor realism, nor is it a theory. Accordingly it is not a theory of explanation of the world, but it is purely and simply a statement of facts- what we are and what we see around us. It voices the phenomenal description of the perplexities and vanities of earthly existence. He observes that good and bad; death and life, happiness and misery are not two opposite existences. The fire that can harm a child can also make a good meal. So there will never be a perfectly good or bad world, because the very idea is a contradiction in terms. Hence Vivekananda considers the theory of Maya as providing neither an optimistic nor pessimistic view of the world.

While discussing the question of the personal god, Vivekananda's views tally perfectly with Advaita Vedanta. Maya which is the cause of this universe with its manifold objects is also responsible for maintaining a personal god called *Iswara. He* is the same Absolute looked at through the power of Maya.[36] Vivekananda's views could be summarized thus: "When we observe him with the five senses, we can see him only as the personal god. *Iswara* is the highest possible knowing of the Absolute

---

[36] *The Complete Works of Swami Vivekananda*, Vol.3, p. 37.

itself which is viewed relatively in the phenomenal plane".[37] Thus Vivekananda argues that it is only on the superficial point of view the two gods namely 'Para Brahman' or the Absolute God and 'Apara Brahma' or the personal God can be conceived. Para Brahman which cannot be defined other than not this not this is. Apara Brahman has qualities and individuality is transient, finite, dynamic and possessing form. He is conceived as the omniscient, omnipotent and omnipresent God who creates preserves and destroys the universe. Delineating the concepts of Absolutely and personal God, Vivekananda declares, "The same impersonal is conceived by the mind as the creator, the preserver and the dissolver of the universe its material as well as its efficient cause the supreme ruler, the being or the loving, the beautiful in the highest sense".[38] The sameness of Brahman and *Iswara* is presented with an illustration.[39] He describes: If a man ventures out on a journey to the sun he will find it becoming bigger and bigger, until he reaches the real one. At each stage of his progress he apparently seemed a different sun, yet it was the same sun he was seeing all the while. Thus Vivekananda concludes that personal God is nothing but the personalized Impersonal Absolute.

---

[37] G.N. Sharma, *Tradition and Change: A Study of Twentieth Century Indian Thought* (Delhi: Kaveri Books, 1994), p. 99.

[38] *The Complete Works of Swami Vivekananda*, Vol.5, p. 336.

[39] *ibid.*, p. 224.

Concept of Man

In accordance with the Vedantic metaphysics, Vivekananda states man is more than what constitute of his physical self. The 'Real Man' as he called is that human being who is perfectly identified with the universal divine spirit. He favoured and quoted in many occasions the Upanisadic *mahavakya* '*Tat-tvam-as*i' (Thou art that) to explain the identity of Brahman with the individual soul.[40] But he points out the reality that in spite of the divine nature, man remains ignorant of the same. Vivekananda calls such a person "apparent man" who has become alienated from his own divinity and spiritual oneness and ponders himself as a part of nature with his weaknesses and imperfections. It is due to ignorance that the truths of his oneness with God remain concealed to him. He deplores "Not knowing our real nature which is perfection, we chase imperfections and waste our substance. If our actions are imperfect and entail infinite sorrow, it is because we crave for the unsubstantial, unaware of our inner plentitude.[41]

Every soul according to him is infinite if it is not touched by space, time and causation. He says that infinite power and infinite purity are present all the same in a worm and in the noblest saint.[42] The difference lies only in the degree of manifestation. With the help of several traditional metaphors Vivekananda illustrate

---

[40] Swami Vivekananda, *Advaita Vedanta: The Scientific Religion*, p. 49.

[41] Swami Jyothirmayananda, *Vivekananda: His Gospel of Man Making* (Madras : Sakti,1986), p.157.

[42] Swami Vivekananda, *Advaita Vedanta: The Scientific Religion*, p. 24.

the error in the individualization of selves. He speaks of individual souls as the reflection (*pratibimba*) of the Infinite which are like reflections of the sun on globules of water appears to be millions of suns.[43] Each globule shows a miniature picture of the sun. Likewise all souls are but reflections and not real. The reflection might be in accordance with the clarity and obscureness of the reflecting surface. So does the reflection of the Infinite as human self vary with the degree of opaqueness of '*avidya*'

In agreement with Vedanta philosophy Vivekananda considers human body to be comprised of two types of bodies *sthulasarira* (physical body) and *sukshma sarira* (subtle body).[44] The gross body can be perceived through senses while the subtle body is composed of the internal sense, the motor organs vital elements and the internal mechanism of knowledge (*antakarana*).[45] Both these bodies, he states undergo continual changes, man experience the existence of something which coordinates and prevails as an unchanging principle within him. It is because of *avidya* or nescience, the soul erroneously associates itself with the gross and subtle bodies, resulting in bondage.

Yogas for Liberation

Vivekananda proclaims that relieving oneself from *avidya* and thereby from bondage is the purpose of human life. For rising to the level of Absolute by realising the innate nature, one has to advance in the way of true knowledge. Social growth

---

[43] *The Complete Works of Swami Vivekananda*, Vol.3, p.7.

[44] *The Complete Works of SwamiVivekananda*, Vol.2, p. 424.

[45] Thomas Mannummel S.J, *op.cit.*, p.123.

depends on individual growth and perfection it in the subjective world that rules the objective. Change the subject and the object is bound to be charged; purity yourself, and the world is bound to be purified.[46] Thus Vivekananda suggested that it is not by intellectual conviction, but by the personal exertions through *abhyasa* and *vairagya*, man can attain purity and thereby part take in the modification of society. *Vairagya* indicates non- attachment to life and *abhyasa* suggests the constant practice of anyone of the yogas. He recognizes the importance of all the different ways of realising the Truth. The one ultimate goal of the realisation of the God within man can be reached through the diverse methods of *karma, bhakti, jnana* and *raja yoga*. He claimed that the *yogas* are capable of satisfying the spiritual quest of a person in accordance with the capacity of his mind. There are different types of individuals and one man's meat is ever so often another man's poison. In practice each yoga is related to one of the four main categories of human nature- the active the emotional, the mystic and the philosophical according to which one chooses an appropriate method to realize his goal.[47] These paths were meant to attain personal liberation in the Hindu tradition. But Vivekananda interpreted them as means to attain social liberation also. The goal of all the *yogas* is to control and break off the 'false ego' which hinders man from progress, both individual and social .*Yoga* furnishes the comprehensive system of methods for all humanity to reach oneness. Vivekananda said, "What I want to propagate is a religion that will be equally acceptable to all minds; it must be equally philosophic,

---

[46] *The Complete Works of SwamiVivekananda*, Vol.1, p. 426.
[47] *ibid.*, p.385-6.

equally emotional, equally mystic and equally conductive to action".[48] He found that each yoga develops with different emphases but ends in the same goal.

Raja-Yoga

Through *rajayoga*, Vivekananda wanted to offer to humanity a practical and scientifically worked out method of reaching the truth. The observation of method of external world is an easy task as there are many instruments invented for the purpose, but to know the nature of mind and thought of main which are internal seems to be much difficult. The science of *rajayoga*, systematized by the sage Patanjali, is intended as a means of observing the internal states of man by turning the mind inwardly.[49] Thus it recommends on the psycho-physiological method for the practice of self control concentration and meditation by means of which the truth of the divine self is experienced directly

The *yoga* helps to develop mental power to control the mind and allows one to concentrate the mind to discover the innermost recesses of our own minds and experience the infinite knowledge. The power of the mind when it is concentrated, it will illumine, Vivekananda holds this are an effective means of knowledge, which helps one know about the terminal truth regarding God, souls etc.

---

[48] *The Complete Works of Swami Vivekananda*, Vol.2, p. 387.

[49] Swami Vivekananda, *Conquering the Internal Nature: Raja-Yoga* (Kolkata: Advaita Ashrama, 2009), p.7.

Raja yoga as a psychological yoga includes not only physical but mental training also. If the mind is simply a finer part of the body, and that the mind acts upon the body there it follows that the body must react upon the mind. Hence Vivekananda warns that when one's body becomes weak, it will affect his mind and vice versa.[50] He suggests that one needs some physical help in order to control the mind. The manipulation of mind can be obtained through the sufficiently controlled body.[51] An uncontrolled and unguided mind will pull down while a controlled and guided mind will keep man get rid of all pains.

Vivekananda asserts that the external world is the gross form of the internal or the subtle. The finer is always the cause, the grosser, the effect, the internal, the cause. A man who has discovered and learned to manage the internal force can easily control the whole of nature. The mind, he says is an instrument in the hands of the soul through which the soul knows the external objects the mind which is constantly changing may attach itself to several organs. A perfected mind holds Vivekananda, can attach all the organs simultaneously as it has the reflexive power to know all the different mental states.[52]

As science requires certain practices which must be followed before it could be understood, so is the case with *rajayoga*. Vivekananda suggests certain regulations in food habits as the food which one takes may affect the mind. All the forces that are

---

[50] Swami Vivekananda, *Raja-yoga*, p.11.

[51] *ibid.*, p.12.

[52] *The Complete Works of Swami Vivekananda*, Vol.1, p.136.

working in one's body are being produced out of the food one eats. So he insists that one needs to take care of the food he eats until he is strong enough to withstand all attacks which hamper his spiritual perfections.[53] But he was against for turning of one's body by fasting which will cause physical weakness and thereby leads to a weak mind.[54] A *yogi* must refrain from the two extremes of luxury and austerity. Instead of extreme fasting and torture of one's flesh a middle path is prescribed. Accordingly one who fasts, one who works too much and one who does not do any work can never be a *yogi*.[55] The teachings of the Gita and the Buddha uphold a view which is similar to the aforesaid one.

Raja yoga is divided into eight steps during the first two stages, i.e. *yama* and *niyama* means has to go through ethical training. *Yama* comprises of the "the shall nots" of yoga. The novice is to refrain from injury of thought, word or deed, from falsehood (satya), covetousness, *(asteya),* and passion, lust and from receiving gifts *(aparigraha)*. Vivekananda says that even when a man receives a gift from another person, he loses his independence and becomes bound and attached.[56] Next is *niyama* which stands for regular habits and observances.The positive qualities or habits of observances, contentment, and austerity study and self-surrender to gold should be cultivated.[57] During the next three stages (*asana, pranayama and pratyahara*) a

---

[53] *idem.*

[54] *idem.*

[55] Swami Vivekananda, *Raja Yoga*, p.18.

[56] Gautam Sen, *op.cit.*, p.139.

[57] *idem.*

person develops the discipline of the body through a series of physical and mental exercises aimed at training and hardening the organism for the higher stages.[58] There is not even a single muscle in the body over which a man cannot establish a perfect control.[59] He holds that even the heart can be made to stop and go on at one's bidding and each part of an organizer can be similarly controlled.

The fourth state *pranayama* has to be achieved with concentrating the power of the mind. It stands for control over prana, the infinite and ornipresent power of the universe. Vivekananda maintains that from thought down to the lowest force everything is manifestation of *prana*.[60] It is the sum total of all the force in the increasing level including mental or physical force, in their original state. Vivekananda say "Breath is like the fly-wheel of this machine, the body. In a big engine you find the flywheel first moving, and that motion is conveyed to finer and finer machinery until the most delicate and trust mechanism in the machine is in motion. The breath is that fly-wheel supplying and regulating the motive power to everything in the body".[61] That part of *pranayama* which attempts to regulate the manifestation of the *prana* by physical means is a physical science and that portion of it which tries to control the manifestation of the *prana* as a mental force by mental

---

[58] Swami Vivekananda, *Rajayoga*, p. 21.

[59] *idem.*

[60] *idem*

[61] *The Complete Works of Swami Vivekananda*, Vol.1, p.143.

means is what Vivekananda call *Raja yoga* [62] He who maintains to control the *prana* can love control over his own mind, and all the minds that exist.

Pratyahara comes next to *pranayama*. Vivekananda says that perception occurs due to the attachment of external instruments and internal organs acting the body through the brain centres and mind, and to some external objects. All the internal and external section over when the mind joins itself with the centre called organs.Willingly or unwillingly mind is drawn to join itself with the centres of perception. That is why people do unwanted deeds and feel miserable. If the mind is under control there he could control his feeling and willing processes. *Pratyahara* meant the stoppage of the outgoing power of the mind, thereby freeing it from the bondage of senses.[63] The *yogi* tries to hold in check all the affective reaction to the external world. Vivekananda avers: "The mind ranges over wide circles of thought and those circle widen out into ever increasing circles, as in a pond when we throw a stone into it .We cannot to reverse the process and starting with a huge circle make it narrower until at last we can fix the mind on one point and make it stay there".[64] This stage which is stepping stone to concentration can be tamed only by patient and continuous practicing.

The next three higher stages namely, *dharana, dhyana* and *samadhi* involve psychical exercises. *Dharana* is the state of confining the *chitta* or mind fix to a

---

[62] Swami Vivekananda, *Raja yoga*, p.33.

63 Amiya.P.Sen, *op.cit.*, p.221.

[64] GautamSen, *op.cit.*, p.148.

constant point.[65] *Dhyana* which follows *dharana* is yogic mediation or one-pointed concentration .*Dhyana* comprises a markedly greater intensity of concentration than the previous two stage .The mind can attain calmness very easily where one practices mediation with anything on which one's mind is most apt to settle down.[66] This is the reason why in India so much worships of the images of gods and goddesses. By telling the story of a king who has obsession towards ornaments was asked by a *yogin* to concentrate his mind on his diamond bracelet in order to attain spiritual perfection, Vivekananda emphasized the above mentioned point.[67] When only this consciousness of object of meditation vanishes, the consciousness of Brahman or *samadhi* can be achieved. *Samadhi* implies the summit of concentration where the subject merges into the object, the union of the knower and the known become possible .The human mind works in two planes according to Vivekananda -conscious and unconscious. In the conscious place all actions are linked up with a feeling of egoism, while in unconscious level, there is no place for egoism. When the mind goes beyond the line of consciousness, *samadhi* or super consciousness state or trance, contemplation can be established. He mentions three levels of consciousness, namely, the unconscious, the conscious and the super-conscious.[68] The activities of lower animals are controlled by the activities of the unconscious mind. It is called instinct. The activities of men

---

[65] Amiya.P.Sen, *op.cit.*, p.225.

[66] Gautam Sen, *op.cit.*, p.149.

[67] *ibid.*, p.150.

[68] Shail Kumari Singh, *Religious and Moral Philosophy of Swami Vivekananda* (NewDelhi: Janaki Prakashan, 1983), p.209.

are guided by conscious mind. The intellect is the guiding principle and egoism prevails in this stage. But when the mind transcends the self-conscious stage, then it goes beyond egoism and is said to be in a super-conscious state or *samadhi*. The illumination from which a man emerges from *samadhi* is a much higher experience than what he gets possibly from reasoning. *Samadhi* by whatever name it may go whether is it the *nirvana* of the Buddha or the Hindu *moksa* or the entrance to the Christian 'Kingdom of heaven' is an experience beyond description.[69] Words and reason exist in the phenomenal existence while the transcendental state is by definition, beyond speech. That is the reason why the extremely practical Buddha embraces silence when asked to describe its nature.

Karma Yoga

The way of *Raja-yoga*, Vivekananda opines, is a different one for many ordinary people who do not have either the ascetic habits or the fortitude to follow such a tough path.[70] Hence Vivekananda presented *Karma-yoga* or path of work as an easier way for attaining liberation particularly for those who are active by temperament. The word *karma* has its origin from the Sanskrit root '*Kr*' which implies the meaning 'to do' and hence *karma* cannot be thought of without action. From the metaphysical side, *karma* means the effects of which our actions were the cause. However, in Vivekananda's point of view *karma* just meant work. Action in itself has no inherent moral qualities, is neither good nor bad. It becomes good or bad

---

[69] Gautam Sen, *op.cit*, p.152.

[70] *The Complete Works of Swami Vivekananda*, Vol.7, p.198.

in accordance with the motive from which it springs. If his motive is selfish, it is bad and if the motive is wholly unselfish and unattached, that action in good.[71] He who works without any motive, neither for money, nor for fame, nor for anything else and out of him will come the power to work in such a manner that will transform the world. Such a man represents the very highest ideal of *Karmayoga*. *Karmayoga* teaches the secret of action of performing work without any selfish interest. Like a man of *sattvic* qualities who maintain a balance between activity and inactivity, Vivekananda carves out from the Gita, a man who possesses equilibrium on action and inaction.[72] An ideal man is one who in the midst of intense activity, finds the silence and solitude of the desert.[73]

Through an analogy Vivekananda tries to explain the consequences of a desirous work. While sipping the honey from a flower, if the honeybee's feet stick to the nectar, it won't be able to fly away.[74] Likewise man must do work unattached, by abandoning the fruits of work the balanced mind attains tranquility but the unsteady mind motivated by greed is trapped in its own reward. But working just for nothing is abstruse and meaningless. Man will not submit himself to any form of drudgery without hitching himself to same moral, emotional, philosophic, or practical ends. He can psychologically abandon the material rewards like fame, prosperity only in the hope of reaping more stable goals. For instance, a person come work out of love for

---

[71] *The Complete Works of Swami Vivekananda*, Vol.1, p.1.

[72] Swami Vivekananda, *Karma-yoga* p.13.

[73] *ibid.*, p.11.

[74] *The Complete Works of SwamiVivekananda*, Vol.2, p.2.

his job as work itself is the reward he is yearning. So the exhortation to detach oneself from any object or work itself implies a motive force- the promise of enlightenment.[75] Hindu scripture conceive of creation as God's play. God has nothing to attain by creation. But this act is also a kind of psychological motivation as it creates a natural affinity towards the work. The act of a poet under inspiration and a sportsman who has found his rhythm while playing can be viewed as work done for its own sake. If we put our whole being to whatever we do and give it our whole attention, then that can remove all our frustration, inefficiency and egoism. *Karmayoga* aims at the attainment of perfect self-abnegation and utter unselfishness. A man will be able to get the best of nature only if he has the power of attaching himself to a thing with all his energy and at the same time has the power to detach him from it whenever he wishes.[76] This self control will tend to produce a mighty will a character which makes a Christ or a Buddha.[77]

The aspiring *karmayogi* is unselfish not because he is indifferent to himself, but because it pleases him to be unselfish. Non-attachment means disinterestedness and not uninterestedness. It is not sluggishness, but intense activity. While we are intensely involved in an action, there will be no actor and no action, there is only acting. There is the absence of self-consciousness when absorbed in an act that constitutes happiness. At the time we are not aware that we are happy, we are too

---

[75] Gautam Sen, *op.cit.*, p.93.

[76] Ajeet Jawed, *op.cit.*, p.14.

[77] *The Complete Works of Swami Vivekananda*, Vol.1, p.33.

absorbed just acting .Everything a man does under compulsion build up attachment.[78] When are attachment has become established, it becomes duty .Vivekananda says that whatever you have to give to the world do give by all means, but not as a duty, because duty implies compulsion. Work without any idea of duty but for its own sake is what Vivekananda advocates.[79]

Corroborating the same idea Vivekananda urges everyone to 'work through freedom' and work through love. Love never comes until there is freedom.[80] There is no true love possible in a slave. He states that a slave who works for his master will work like a drudge, but there will be no love in him. In the like manner when we work ourselves for the things of the world as slaves, there can be no love in us and our work may not be a perfect work. Hence Vivekananda wanted everyone to work like a master and not as a slave.[81] Man must learn to work with perfect mastery.

Vivekananda upholds the Sankhya theory that physical world comprises the three *gunas* or cosmic force namely *sattva*, *rajas* and *tamas*.[82] *Tamas* is typified as inactivity, *Rajas* is activity and *sattva* is the equilibrium of the two. These three forces are present in varying degrees in everyman. Inactivity, dullness and laziness shown by a man may be due to the predominance of *tamoguna*. Men who exhibit the characteristics such as activity, power and manifestation of energy have *rajoguna* and

---

[78] Gautham Sen, *op.cit.*, p.109.

[79] *The Complete Works of Swami Vivekananda*, Vol.1, p.66.

[80] Gautham Sen, *op.cit.*, p.103.

[81] *The Complete Works of Swami Vivekananda*, Vol.1, p.66.

[82] Swami Vivekananda, *Karma Yoga*, p.13.

those who possess *sattvaguna* are full of sweetness, calmness and gentleness which are due to the balancing of both action and inactive. This *karma yoga*, he claims is intended for making everyman a *sattvika* who renounces not action but selfish impulses in action.

Vivekananda added a new dimension to *karmayoga*. He wanted everyone to serve his fellow being not with are attitude of extending help to them. When one serves *jiva* with the idea that he is it out of compassion and not love. But when he is serving others with the idea that he is the self there is love.[83] One must always think of serving others as serving his very self. It is entirely wrong to think that one is doing some help to others. All work that one has done is ultimately for his own benefit. Hence Vivekananda exhorts that everyone should consider it a great privilege to be allowed to do something for this world.

Bhakti-Yoga

Bhakti-yoga in Vivekananda's view point is the path leading to the destruction of bondage and the recovery of man's true nature through the way of the heart. It the easiest and the most natural way to reach the 'Divine'.[84] It is defined as a real, genuine search after god, a search beginning, continuing and ending in love.[85] Vivekananda present three essential characteristic of true love. He says wherever

---

[83] Swami Vivekananda, *Salvation and Service* (Calcutta: Advaita Ashrama, 1998), p.67.

[84] Swami Vivekanada, *Bhakti Yoga*, (Kolkata: Advaita Ashrama, 2009), p.4.

[85] *The Complete Works of Swami Vivekananda*, Vol.3, p.31.

there is any seeking for something in return; there can be no real love. Those who worship God for recurring favors from Him are false *bhaktas*, full of personal desires to seek his own benefit. In true devotion there is a rejection of personal craving. Another feature of a true love is fearlessness.[86] Love knows no fear. It is a degradation to worship God through fear of punishment. When fear persists in one's mind, he cannot love sincerely. The third attribute of a real worshipper as love knows no rival for in it is always embodied the lover's highest ideal.[87] Every person projects her own ideal on the outside world and worships it. Genuine love is free from all bondages and imitations. Vivekananda says that when a person understands the love of God, all the images, temples, churches, religion, sects, nationalities' and all other limitation and bondages become irrelevant to him.[88]

Vivekananda has described how one experiences the divine love. The lowest form in which the love of God is grasped is called the *Santa*. In this state the *bhakta* is perfectly controlled by the divine will. *Santa bhakti* is and peaceful devotion in which one has gone beyond forms and symbols and intensively seeks for God.[89] The next highest type of devotion that Vivekananda talks about is that of '*dasya*' or 'servant ships' where one thinks of oneself as the servant of God.[90] Here the relation between God and man is like that of a faithful servant and his master. *Sakhya* or friendship is

---

[86] *ibid.*, p.88.

[87] *ibid.*, p.89.

[88] Gautan Sen, *op.cit.*, p.183.

[89] *The Complete Works of Swami Vivekananda*, Vol.3, p. 93.

[90] Swami Vivekananda, *Bhakti Yoga*, p.102.

considered as the next type of love where God is regarded as a beloved friend.[91] As there is the idea of equality between him and his friend, the love that flowers between the worshipper and his friendly God assumes a sense of equality. Because of this friendly attitude, he can place before Him the innermost secrets of his heart with great assurance of safety and support. The next type is known as *Vatsalya*[92] in which god is conceived as one's child. While speaking about this conception Vivekananda says of the detachment of the idea of the omnipotence of God. The last type of love that he mentions is the highest of all representations of love which in called *madhurya*.[93] The nature of this love is such that, the more obstruction are there for its play the more passionate it emerges. In this state, the whole universe seems to the devotee as immersed in love. In this delightful state of love there is no thought any more of the petty self.[94] The whole of the nature changes and the universe itself melts away into the one infinite ocean of love. These descriptions suggest that the devotee satisfies his or her emotional feelings. In the final state everything is perceived as a manifestation of God.[95] As a result of this intense all-absorbing love comes the feeling of self-surrender. So human representation of this divine love convey the idea that all loves and all passions of the human heart must find fulfillment in God because God is in

---

[91] *idem.*

[92] *idem.*

[93] Swami Vivekananda, *Bhakti Yoga*, p.106.

[94] *The Complete Works of Swami Vivekananda*, Vol.5, p.73.

[95] *The Complete Works of Swami Vivekananda*, Vol.3, p. 82.

everything.⁹⁶ It also suggests that the "love, the lover and the beloved are one."⁹⁷ Thus the devotee experience no duality between the God of the love and his own self, he sees only the all-encompassing love which embraces the whole of the universe as one.

Vivekananda affirms that man has to begin as a dualist in the *yoga* of love. At first the *bhakta* and the lord are apparently separate. There love comes as bridge through which the man approaches God and God also moves towards man. For Vivekananda this process of closer union progress gradually with the final transportation of the *bhakta* into the relation of super-consciousness. In this stage, the fire love burns the veil of *avidya* and the devotee becomes absolutely merged in the object of worship. Vivekananda through this highest stage of divine union fits the yoga of love into the scheme of Advaita.

Thus Vivekananda demonstrated supreme *bhakti* to be a path by which one can achieve the goal of neo-vedantic ideal of oneness. He aimed to make *bhakti* applicable to many in order to fabricate universal love for solving human problems. He tried to transform the Hindu traditional *bhakti* which aimed only at the individual search of God, neglecting its social relevance into human centered activism.⁹⁸ *Bhakti* is not a way of seeking one's own emotional satisfaction, but rather a way of liberation for oneself and for others. Vivekananda says that there is no *mukthi* on earth

---

[96] *ibid.*, p.100.

[97] *idem.*

[98] Abraham Stephen, *op.cit.*, p.208.

to call one's own. It is only by doing good to others that one attains to one's own good, and it is by leading others to *bhakti* and *mukti* that one attains them oneself.[99]

Jnana Yoga

Jnanayoga is a way which is strictly in conformity with the doctrine of Advaita. It is the rational method which follows the way of knowledge to realize the divine self. He defined its methodical discipline in the following way: "The *jnana-yogi* forces his way to the realization of God by the power of pure reason. He must be prepared the throw away all old idols, all old belief and superstitions, all desires for this world or another, and be determined only find freedom".[100] The true knowledge of reality can be attained by the elimination of ignorance. The devotee realises his nature only when his ignorance is removed. A *jnani* has to realize "I am not the body, I am not the mind, I am not thought, I am not even consciousness, I am the *Atman*".[101] So a *jnani* has to transcend unreality and must realise his real self which is imperishable. This can be achieved only by the proper understanding of the vedantic truths.

Vivekananda has described the four preparatory stages which the student should pass through before undertaking the vedantic study. The first and foremost mark of a *jnana-yogi* is the ability to discriminate between what is eternal and what is

---

[99] *The Complete Works of Swami Vivekananda*, Vol.6, p.266.

[100] *The Complete Works of Swami Vivekananda*, Vol.8, p.3.

[101] *The Complete Works of Swami Vivekananda*, Vol.8, p.4.

transitory.¹⁰² That is he should be a rationalist who takes nothing for granted and analyses everything by pure reason and force of will. Then comes '*shama*' (tranquility) and '*dama*' (control of senses) which means keeping the various organs in their respective center without allowing there to stray out and restraining the mind from wanderings outward or inward.¹⁰³ Then the *jnana yogi* must possess *titiksha* (forbearance) a state of mind in which one is calm even in a difficult situation, without any feeling of hatred, anger or any thought of resistance .The next step Vivekananda discusses is *uparati* (withdrawl) which means not thinking of things of the senses. Here he wants not the abandonment of the worldly pleasures as such to be in the world and to be not it is the true test of a *sannyasin*.¹⁰⁴ Another requirement of a true *jnani* is *sraddha* or faith. It constitutes a strong faith in God and the consequent eagerness to reach Him. Then comes *samadhana* (one-pointedness of mind) which is constant practice to stick the mind in God. The last of the preparatory stages is the *mumukshutva*, the earnest desire to be free without any attachment. He must know the vanity in pleasure and must be detached from everything, except God as the free divine self.

The above mentioned qualities are essentially a discipline for the purification of the heart so that oneness with can be realized .One the preparations are over the

---

[102] Romain Rolland, *The World Religion of Vivekananda* (Delhi: Vijay Goel, 2005), p.60.

[103] *The Complete Works of Swami Vivekananda*, Vol.1, p. 406.

[104] Amiya.P.Sen, *The Indispensable Vivekananda*, *op.cit.*, p.229.

aspirant must listen to the vedantic teaching from a *guru (sravana)*.[105] Then he has to think deeply about them and understand through reasoning which is termed *manana*.[106] Then comes constant meditation on these Truths and realise them until at last they become his whole life. This stage is called *nidhidyasana*. When the man realizes the super conscious state by controlling his mind, he feels the divine nature within himself.

According to Vivekananda, the *jnani's* constant practice of *yoga* is not to withdraw from the society but rather that, having realised the divine nature, he might guide it in the right path: "The true *Jnani* is he who has the deepest love with in his heart and at the same time is a practical seer of Advaita in his outward relations".[107] A *jnani* must love and act in a perfectly unattached way in the society.

Vivekananda states that knowledge is the goal of all life. It is through knowledge that one frees oneself from bondage. Without knowing the real nature of divinity, man considers himself as weak and helpless, which will fasten him to bondage. Only when the knowledge of divinity is revealed to oneself, the delusion and ignorance will vanish. He has to lose sight of variety and see only the unity. The *jnana yogi* has to be free from all forms; he is rather a Hindu nor a Buddhist, nor a Christian. Man can achieve transcendence of group-bound religiosity and lifted the

---

[105] Swami Vivekananda, *Jnana yoga*, p.398.

[106] *idem*.

[107] *The Complete Works of Swami Vivekananda*, Vol.5, p. 318.

pilgrim to the plane of universality[108] through the practice of yoga. By the practice of these *yogas* one can become secular and spiritual at the same time. The aim and end of a *jnani* is to become a *jivan-muktah*, who is living free while living. He can live in this world without being attached to it. Vivekananda asserts that even after realising his oneness with the entire universe the work of the individual is not over; he has to continue to be in the world, living in the society and helping his fellowmen in making their lives healthier and purer. His ideal of mass liberation has a clear similarity with the Buddhist ideal of Bodhisattva which was mentioned in the earlier chapter. But it differs from that of Aurobindo and S.Radhakrishna when they say that the attainment of individual immortality is not the ultimate human destiny and the goal pursued must be redemption of all. "By my own efforts knowledge, love and service- I may realize immortality. I may show the way to others also, but he can realize immortality only through his own efforts,"[109] says Vivekananda. Thus though Vivekananda does not accept the view that redemption would be final only when a universal redemption is achieved, he urged every realized soul to help others in their spiritual growth, even after attaining realization.

Vivekananda prophesied that the conclusion which the Advaita Vedanta will find authentication in modern science. This has come true when the New Physics discovered that the world can no longer be looked upon as a conglomeration of isolated blocks but should be looked upon as interpretation of Cosmic Energy through

---

[108] Swami Jyothirmayananda, *op.cit.*, p.121.

[109] Basant Kumarlal, *Contemporary Indian Philosophy* (Delhi: Motilal Banarsidass, 1973), p. 30.

matter, life and mind. Vivekananda's observation that Science and Religion are not opposed because while the former discovers unity in the outer world the latter seeks unity in the inner world. Advaita accepts the challenge of holding man at his highest in his essential nature. Once this is realized man's attainment of self-fulfilment become easy.

Vivekananda's views on Vedanta and the paths for the realisation of God are worthwhile and practical. He wrote to his disciple about his mission and motivation to make out the philosophy of Advaita and perverted mythology to a thought which shall be popular and at the same time helps to meet the requirements of the highest mind. He said: "The dry abstract Advaita must become living-poetic in everyday life: out of hopelessly intricate mythology must come concrete moral forms; and out of bewildering *yogism* must come the most scientific and practical psychology and all this must be put in a form so that a child may grasp it. That is my life's work."[110] He had brought the ancient philosophy of the Vedic sages back to our home, our city and our society; it is a guide to our life and conduct, an outlook that may energize our individual social, national and international life.[111] This Vedantic ideal of divinity and solidarity of man provides the stable foundation for his social thought. However, Vivekananda cannot be regarded as a system builder as he writes no treatise on philosophical, spiritual, social or political matters. But he identified the basic maladies and weaknesses of Indian society and suggested remedies for them.

---

[110] *The Complete Works of Swami Vivekananda*, Vol.5, pp.104-5.

[111] R.C.Majumdar, ed., *Swami Vivekananda, Centuary Memorial Volume* (Calcutta: Ramakrishna Mission, 1963), p.281.

CHAPTER IV

SOCIAL IDEAS OF VIVEKANANDA

In the pursuit of 'socio-spiritualism' Vivekananda has attempted to reorient the traditional Indian spiritualism to meet the demands of modern society. Instead of preaching 'other-worldliness', this new spiritualism affirms life and discourages indifference to socio-political activities. It is alertness of the inescapable entanglement of man with his socio-cultural and economic-political surroundings.[1] His socio-spiritualistic approach has its base in the Vedanta conception of solidarity in the universe which creates the feeling of oneness that leads to social commitment. Vedanta, states Vivekananda, which has so far been applied only on spiritual plane has to be extended to the daily practical life. The Vedanta teaching that envisages no ultimate difference between man and man, promotes to foster a humanistic and peaceful social living. It states that the same omnipresent, omniscient soul resides in every man and in every animal.[2] It gives the impression that a divine principle is the common substance of this universe which makes everyone feel the oneness with it. This shifting of God from a far-off heaven to the heart of every being as his innermost self marks a significant advance in the spiritual history of the world.

---

[1] D.P. Chattopadhyaya, ed., *Essays in Social and Political Philosophy* (New Delhi: ICPR in association with Allied Publishers, 1989), p.625.

[2] Swami Vivekananda, *The Complete Works of Swami Vivekananda* (Kolkata: Advaita Ashrama, 2003), Vol.3, p.126.

Neo-Vedanta Thought- Synthesis of Theory and Practice

The social thought of Vivekananda mainly rests on the metaphysical teachings of Vedanta with its ideal of solidarity and divinity of man. His desire for its practical application among all men is rightly revealed when he says: "That society is greatest where highest truth become practical. And if society is not fit for the highest truth, make it so- the sooner the better". [3] Vivekananda wanted the realm of Vedanta to be extended to the daily practical life of man. Following his master's teachings, he has turned the Vedantic ideals useful for humanity in satisfying the spiritual as well as the social needs of it. The conception of oneness of the divine spirit is also the case of his ideal of social morality. In accordance with its ideal, he recommends universal selfhood rather than universal brotherhood. This will contribute to the view that every action will affect the organic unity of human life: "In hurting anyone you hurt yourself and in loving any one you love yourself".[4] In such a deeply integrated cosmic life-vision every action tends to produce a great impact just like a wave in the ocean. This social morality reminds us that no other power except the spiritual solidarity is able to produce such a strong application of social concern because it holds that "I am the same as any other man, as any animal... It is one body, one mind, one soul throughout."[5] This understanding leads to a further understanding that

---

[3] Swami Adiswarananda, *Vivekananda World Teacher: His Teachings on the Spiritual Unity of mankind* (New Delhi: Rupa Publications India Pvt. Ltd., 2007), p.xvii.

[4] Mohit Chakraborthi, *Swami Vivekananda: Excellence in Education* (Delhi: Kalpaz Publication, 2008), p.87.

[5] *The Complete Works of Swami Vivekananda*, Vol.8, p.129.

humanitarianism is a divine dimension. It is this deep-rooted interconnection that makes one aware of the interdependency in social life.

Vivekananda has promoted spiritual humanism that renders loving service to the Divine, seeing its presence in all beings. He wants to impress upon the people that working for others should not be considered as a mere charity rather; it should be regarded as a privilege that one gets. In his opinion the poor and the miserable are giving man the opportunity to serve God coming to him in the person of the diseased, the lunatic, the leper and the sinner.[6] It is this conviction that inspired him to say "May I be born again and again and suffer thousands of miseries so that I may worship the only God that exists, the only God I believe in, the sum total of all souls- and above all my God the wicked, my God, the miserable, my God, the poor of all races, of all species is the special object of my worship."[7] Here his sayings echo the views of his master Sri Ramakrishna who was always willing to accept any sort of bodily pain or even death if that could bring a single soul to salvation.[8] Thus by the knowledge of Reality made one to engage in altruistic and socially constructive work. By rendering service it is not the receiver but the giver that is blessed. This might be the reason why he makes the call: "Be thankful that you are allowed to exercise the

---

[6] Eastern and Western Admirers, *Reminiscences of Swami Vivekananda* (Kolkata: Advaita Ashrama, 2004), p.101.

[7] Swami Vivekananda, *Thoughts of power*, (Kolkata: Advaita Ashrama, 2008), p.23.

[8] Max Muller, *Ramakrishnan: His life and sayings* (London: Longmans, Green and Co., 1898), p.57.

power of benevolence and mercy in the world and thus become pure and perfect".[9] He believed that if one looks upon other human beings as God, one cannot help but serve him without desiring for any return. Here the server can serve mankind selflessly without the sense of ego. Here he combines both humanism and humanitarianism. He tries to give to his philosophy a humanistic garb recommending humanitarian work and service.[10]

Vivekananda has viewed religion as a process of evolution of dynamic faith towards spiritual destiny. He believes that in India, the ideals of renunciation and service have been handed down to posterity without any break through various religious ceremonies and festivals in which acts of charity play an important role. Realising the fact that religion as the base of all socially constructive programmes in India, he says: "... the life of this nation is religion, its language religion, and its idea religion; and your politics, society, municipality, plague-prevention work, and famine-relief work-all these things will be done as they have been done all along here, viz., only through religion."[11] Revealing his mind he opines that politics and social reform divorced from religion would do lasting and effective benefit to India. He added: "Only a spontaneous development from inside, following an ancient tradition,

---

[9] D.R.Jatava, *Evolution of Indian Social Thought* (Jaipur: Bohra Publications, 1987), p.206.

[10] Basant Kumarlal, *Contemporary Indian Philosophy* (Delhi: Motilal Banarsidass, 1973), p.XVII.

[11] *Vivekananda : His call to the Nation*: A Compilation (Kolkata: Advaita Ashrama, 2009), p.81.

could lift India". [12] Hence he advised to overwhelm India with spiritual ideas than filling it with the heartless foreign politics of other countries. He was convinced that political or social evolution is not possible unless it has its base in religion.

However, Vivekananda was not unaware that religious fanaticism, born of narrow outlook had resulted in conflict and war throughout history. Hence he held that all narrow, limited fighting ideas of religion must be given up. During his lectures in India and abroad, he consistently delivered a message of universal religion, which opens its gate to every individual. When he states that it is not the truth, but it is ultimately left to one's inner likes and choices that determine his religion, it gets universalized.[13] His concept of universal religion supersedes the conflicts between different sects and appears reasonable to them all. His concept of universal religion is a mixture of spirituality of the Hindus, the mercifulness of the Buddhists, the activity of the Christians and the brotherhood of the Mohammedans in practical life.[14] Accordingly for him the religion is not mere talk or doctrine, theories or sectarianism nor it consist in erecting temples or building churches or attending public worship or in lectures or in organizations.[15] But for him the religion has its scope centered in humanity to realize its own true divine nature; the means to manifest the

---

[12] Eastern and Western Admirers, *op.cit.*, p. 403.

[13] Basant Kumarlal, *op.cit.*, p.43.

[14] *The Complete Works of Swami Vivekananda*, Vol .8, pp.79-80.

[15] Bimal Prasad ,ed., *Swami Vivekananda: An Anthology SwamiVivekanandaSelectedSpeeches and Writings* (New Delhi : Vikas Publishing House, 1994), p.42.

quintessential in man. It is a question of being and becoming, not of merely believing.[16] To quote him: "Thus my religion means expansion and expansion means realization and perception in the highest sense- no mumbling words or genuflection".[17] Dr. Radhakrishnan also held a similar position while he presents religion as an experience in which every aspect of man's being is raised to its highest extent rather than of pure intellectual conformity or ceremonial piety.[18] Thus Vivekananda gives a new meaning to religion. He not only humanized it, but also socialized its purposes.

Concept of Universal Religion- Harnessing of Different Paths

Vivekananda's concept of Universal Religion has developed from his rational approach to the Vedantic idea of Divinity that manifests everywhere. Every religion reveals the same truth that God is within man. Hence he upholds equal validity to all religions and holds the view that no one religion has a monopoly of truth. As is said in the Vedic literature, it can be noticed that St. Paul the greatest exponent of Christianity tells us the same thing while he writes, "know you not that you are the temple of God and the spirit of God dwelt in you".[19] Islam also conveys the same

---

[16] *The Complete Works of Swami Vivekananda*, Vol .4, p.216.

[17] *The Complete Works of Swami Vivekananda*, Vol.1, p.32.

[18] *President Radhakrishnan's Speeches and Writings* (New Delhi: Director, Publication Division, Patalia House, 1969), p.375.

[19] New Testament, 1 Corinthians 3:16

message that God is near to man than his own jugular vein.[20] If we overlook the divine spark which we all possesses we will become bound to things, ideas and abstractions. Thus he symbolized communal peace and harmony on universal acceptance and respect for all faiths. In today's world, there are various religions conflicting with one another and most people think that his or her opinion as the only perfect and acceptable view of religion to be followed. Vivekananda realizes the reason for these religious conflicts as man's ignorance regarding the meaning of a true religion.

Though Vivekananda recommended the acceptance of all religions, he does not mean that a person have to observe the rites and rituals of other's religion. All that it implies is that one has to enrich his own religion by assimilating whatever is of abiding value in other religions. It was in accordance with his Master's precept, *Jato mat, tato path*,[21] he recommended the acceptance of variety of forms of beliefs. This serves as the basis of his Universal Religion. Here he does not try to assimilate the ideals of different religions of the world, but only to implement a new approach to discover the universality behind world's existing religions.

---

[20] Quran50:16 cited in Paramjit Singh Sachdeva, *Appreciating All Religions* (Bloomington: Author House, 2011), p.116.

[21] As there are a number of beliefs, there are a number of ways.

The social tinge in his concept of religion distinguishes him from other nineteenth century thinkers. He has drawn practical lessons in relation to the matters concerning religion by liberating religion from the label of mere theory or an intellectual consent. Two attempts in the world have been recognized by him to initiate a social life: the one was upon religion, and the other was upon social necessity.[22] Religion which does not aim the improvement of the social condition of the poor and the suppressed could not claim to be called religion at all. Thus the principal lesson of religion according to Vivekananda consists in service to God in the form of care and concern for all sentient worlds. He said, "So long as even a single dog in my country is without food my whole religion will be to feed it."[23] Again he wrote "I do not believe in a god or religion which cannot wipe the widow's tears or bring a piece of bread to the orphan's mouth".[24] He added that he cannot accept a religion merely confined to books and dogmas even if it has the most sublime theories and well spun philosophy.[25] It was the lesson that he inherited from Sri Ramakrishna made him remark that an empty stomach cannot comprehend the true spirit of religion[26]. Thereby he tried to diminish the distinction between sacred and secular. Regarding this Sister Nivedita writes about his fervour thus: To labour is to pray and

---

[22] Swami Vivekananda, *State, Society and Socialism* (Calcutta: Advaita Ashrama, 1989), p.27.

[23] SantinathChattopadyay, ed., *op.cit.*, p.134.

[24] *The Complete Works of Swami Vivekananda*, Vol.5, p.50.

[25] *Idem.*

[26] Gwilym Beckerlegge, *The Ramakrishna Mission, The Making of a Modern Hindu Society* (New Delhi: Oxford University Press, 2000), p.90.

to conquer is to renounce.[27] Thus he tried to conjoin the individual quest of salvation and spiritual realization which remained exclusive to the realm of religion with the social emancipation.

Thoughts on Eastern Spiritualism and Western Materialism

Vivekananda advocated a synthesis of materialism and spiritualism as he did in the case of theory and practice. He felt that the crying need in the East is not religion, but bread for poor. He holds: "The human being must be ensured of minimum economic security in order to pursue his spiritual goal of god realization undisturbed by anxiety and care".[28] Here lies the economic contend of his philosophy. He hoped that Western material civilization can raise the poor in India from material scarcity. He added that in order to meet the needs of a modern developing society; Indians should learn mechanism[29] and science of physical nature[30] from the West. During his reply to a welcome address in Calcutta, he said, "We can learn mechanism from them. We can learn many other things. But we have to teach them something, and that is out religion that is our spirituality....Therefore we must go out, exchange our spirituality for anything they have to give us; for the marvel of the religion of spirit we will exchange the marvel of the religion of matter... There cannot be friendship without equality, and there cannot be equality

---

[27] *The Complete Works of Swami Vivekananda*, Vol. I, p.XV.

[28] P.Parameswaran, *Marx and Vivekananda* (London: Oriental University Press, 1987), p.38.

[29] *The Complete Works of Swami Vivekananda*, Vol.3, p.317.

[30] *ibid.*, p.443.

when one party is always the teacher and the other party sits always at his feet. If you want to become equal with the English man or the Americans, you will have to teach as well as learn and you have plenty yet to teach to the world for centuries to come."[31] Thus he adopted a give and take policy.

Vivekananda was aware of the demerits of Western Materialistic approach to life. The western society mainly concentrated on external comforts through the development of science and technology. Hence he raised criticism on their exclusive dependence on secular needs rather than spiritual. He felt that the Western society lacked a stable foundation on spirituality.[32] The West cannot ignore the fact that its interest in religion is at low ebb as it totally ignored Christ's life of renunciation and did not reckon his high teachings on the unity and divinity. He characterized the West as excelling in material power and the knowledge of the material world, while the East excelled in spiritual knowledge and power.[33] The West is materialistic in its outlook while the society of the East has its base on spirituality. Thus his criticism of the East of its antipathy of material civilization is paralleled by his severe criticism of modern western attitude towards religion.

---

[31] *The Complete Works of Swami Vivekananda*, Vol.3, pp.317-8.

[32] Sivaramakrishna and SumitaRoy, ed., *Perceptives on Ramakrishna- Vivekananda Vedanta tradition* (NewDelhi: Sterling Publishers Pvt. Ltd., 1991), p.197.

[33] *The Complete Works of Swami Vivekananda*, Vol.4, p.156.

Individualistic Approach of the West and Socialistic Approach of the East

The polarity of East and West, orient and occident, is expressed in various ways in Vivekananda works. He made an analysis on the social freedom enjoyed by the people of the West and also the social system of India with all its restrictions and points out the Western method as individualistic, giving opportunity to the lowest in society. He reiterated that the western man is individualistic while the Hindu is socialistic.[34] There is no freedom for individual unless he becomes a renunciate. In India, the individual had to obey the social rules; he needs to be fit into the system at any cost because of its emphasis on society's good than on the individual's. As freedom is the only condition for growth is restricted for individuals except for renunciates, Indian society could produce only a few immense individualities while the common masses remain deplorably unprogressive state. As freedom is the indispensable condition of growth and development; he realized that its exercise in the Western society provides ample opportunities to its masses.[35] Actually he wanted to remain as an advocate of both, individualism and socialism while envisaging his ideal society.

The West had provided with an ample freedom to the individual in its social structure. Because of the freedom granted to society, there appeared is dynamic

---

[34] *The Complete Works of Swami Vivekananda*, Vol.3, p.62.

[35] Eastern and Western Admirers, *op.cit.*, p.218-9.

growth in Western society, but religious values experienced a progressive degradation. On the other hand the Indian civilization provided every liberty to the soul, so its religion grew, but the society remains static. In Western society, he observed, the values which the religion projected, experienced a progressive degradation.[36] Westerners were much concerned with the external world, giving prominence to politics and social improvement. At the same time the eastern culture is rich with its spiritual ideas. Analyzing the disparity in the conceptions of God and religion he said that in the East, the masses may be ignorant about party politics and economics but not in spiritual matters even if it may be mythological, scriptural or philosophical.[37] But the European ploughman he will prove that he knows much about the matters of party politics, commerce or trade, though he knows little about his religion.[38] The European approach to religion which quite different from that of the East, is sectarian and carnal, while the East treats spiritual realities as things that can be seen and felt. Vivekananda weighed weaknesses of Eastern and Western societies in the secular sphere also. In Indian society, there exists oppressive priest craft while in the West there exist its shylocks.[39] Indian widows are sentenced to life long servitude; the despondency of the unmarried maidens makes the western society

---

[36] Chaturvedi Badrinath, *Swami Vivekananda; The Living Vedanta* (NewYork: Penguin Books, 2006), p.199.

[37] Swami Vivekananda, *State, Soceity and Socialism* , p.7.

[38] William Radice, ed., *Swami Vivekananda and the Modernization of Hinduism* (Calcutta:Oxford University Press,1998), p.138.

[39] S.S.Mittal, *The Social and Political Ideas of SwamiVivekananda* (New Delhi: Metropolitian Book Co. Pvt. Ltd, 1979), p.87.

gloomy.[40] Similarly he wanted the West of make advancement in spiritual realm along with secular and scientific one.

As a close observer of social issues he pointed out the demerits of conservatism and blind imitation of the West. He criticized the spell of imitating the West without reason and also blind discrimination or deference to the scriptures. By pointing out that what is meat for a society or a nation may be poison for the other, he brings to light the futility of pursuing the lines of action that foreign societies have adopted. With sarcasm he questions the Indian's attitude of accepting all that the Westerners admire and rejecting whatever things they dislike or censure. Indians, captivated by the European paradigms had adopted the western social ideals considering it as the only way to be progressive. The misunderstanding that what are western are modern and the consequent westernization in the name of modernization would destroy the sublimities of social structure India has been preserving down the centuries. Vivekananda opines that these spokesmen of modernity are quite uninformed about the essentials of traditional Indian social ideas. As there exist a wide divergence between the western and eastern societies as regards the primitive course and goal, any sect in India framed after the western model will miss its aim.

---

[40] M.B.Chande, *Indian Philosophy in Modern Times* (New Delhi: Atlantic Publishers and Distributors, 2000), p.315.

Hence he realized that both "the Scylla of old orthodoxy and the Charybdis of modern European civilization" are obstacles for the advancement of Indian society.[41]

His philosophy of life is synthetic in character; it lays equal emphasis on material and spiritual aspects in an ideal society. Such a society which recognizes and harmonizes matter and spirit, regrets he, is equally missing in the East and in the West. But that does not constitute a reason for the whole sale condemnation of either society. To say as Marx does: no progress without contradiction that is the law which civilization has obeyed up to this day[42] seems to be an arbitrary statement for Vivekananda. The oriental ideal is a necessity for the progress of the human race as is the occidental. He held that both idealism and realism are complementary to each other.[43] A complete civilization needs a suitable blending of two elements.[44] He said, "My idea as to the key note of our national downfall is that we do not mix with other nations – that is the one and the sole cause. We never had opportunity to compare notes."[45] He felt the necessity to compare the Eastern and Western ideas and to adopt a social and political system which synthesized what is best in the Western tradition and the perennial Indian thought. This showed his vision regarding the importance of exchange of intellectual and social ideas for the proper development of society. Both

---

[41] Swami Vivekananda, *To the Youth of India* (Kolkata: Advaita Ashrama, 2007), p.21.

[42] Amiya.P.Sen, *op.cit.*, p.20.

[43] Siva Ramakrishna and Sumita Roy, ed., *op.cit.*, p.188.

[44] S.Radhakrishnan, *Religion and Society* (London: George Allen and Unwin Ltd., 1959), p.32.

[45] *The Complete Works of Swami Vivekananda*, Vol.5, p.220.

the East and West have to supply and hand down for the accomplishment of an ideal and harmonious society. Though Vivekananda stood in the way of conservatism and blind imitation of the West, he is of the opinion that no individual or nation can live by holding itself separate from the company of others.[46] If any country wants to raise itself it is necessary to bring out its treasures and throws them broadcast among the nations of the earth and in return be ready to receive what others have to give them.[47] He is unique in that he is neither in thrall to the ancient nor is willing to discard the whole thing from it. He declares without any doubt that India needs to learn from the West, but the ensuing modernization should not be allowed to sweep everything that is worthy and good in India. Vivekananda advocated the reconciliation of material and spiritual development not only for the future of Indian but also for an ideal society anywhere in the world. But he always maintained the superiority of Indian ideal of spirituality over any other ideals. He said that oriental ideal is as necessary for the progress of the human race as is the occidental.[48] In his own words: "All healthy social changes are the manifestations of the spiritual forces working within, and if these are strong and well adjusted, society will arrange itself accordingly[49]".

---

[46] Amiya.P.Sen, *The Indispensable Vivekananda- An Anthology of Our Times* (New Delhi: Permanent Black, 2006), p.20.

[47] *The Complete Works of Swami Vivekananda*, Vol.4, p.365-6.

[48] *The Complete Works of Swami Vivekananda*, Vol.4, p.155.

[49] Mohit Chakrabarti, *Swami Vivekananda- Vibrant Humanist* (NewDelhi, Kanishka Publication Distributors, 2012), p.39.

In his view, the total repudiation of the Indian customs and social ethos in toto without rational and argumentative analysis of their merits in the given social context is to be avoided. Supporting the tradition, he visualized that the degeneration of India came not because of the laws and customs of the ancients were bad, but because they were not allowed to be carried to their legitimate conclusion. Hence an attempt was being made to rescue the modern man, groping in western halo to restore the lost spirit in him and thereby made him conscious of his heritage, dignity and responsibility. Though Vivekananda looked to the past for inspiration, he did not want to replicate the past. In that way he is the middle path between Gandhiji and Ambedhkar and therefore, balanced and reflective in pursuing the true Indian mean in society. He suggested its readjustment in accordance with the modern conditions.

Synthesis of Tradition and Modernity

Vivekananda wanted to connect the social, cultural and spiritual values of ancient India to meet the requisites of the modern times. It is the unique feature of any social thought to comprehend the unity underlying the apparent diversity by seeking continuity of the present with the past in which it is rooted and its projection into the future. [50] That is the reason why he finds consonance with the classification of society on the scheme of *Varnasrama dharma* actuated and guided by the four *purusharthas*. Through this unique feature of Indian social scheme, his thought aimed for the provision of a qualitative and healthy social life.

---

[50] K.M.Kapadia, *Marriage and Family in India* (Delhi: Oxford University Press), p.14.

Vivekananda's thought has taken up the four-fold pursuits in the Vedic social organization for the spiritual and social upheavel in human life. While emphasising spirituality and spiritual development of the individual, it does not turn its face towards material advancements. The fulfilment of the basic economic needs and performance of socio-economic duties nevertheless have their place in the overall scheme of life. His social thought maintains that *artha* and *kama* are to be gained on the basis of *dharma* with the aim of attaining *moksha*. *Dharma* and *moksha* are the means and goals of spiritual culture and are necessary for the proper functioning of the social order. The moral value (*dharma*) and the spiritual value (*moksha*) should guide the economic value (*artha*) and the psycho-biological value (*kama*). Some level of material prosperity and the enjoyment of ordinary pleasure of life are necessary for individual and social development. But being stagnant at the level of organic pleasure and satisfaction is to be avoided[51]. At the same time he held that material prosperity which is already recommended in Vedic religion should not be condemned. Rather material prosperity is viewed as friend and not the foe of spiritual regeneration. Vivekananda held that only a society with some level of material prosperity can think about spiritual development and be introspective.

Vivekananda's decisive analysis on both modern thoughts and ancient scriptural texts is exceptional and his capability of drawing apt practical lessons from them is unparallel. In relation to the questions on caste and religion it is striking to

---

[51] Swami Ranganathananda, *Vedanta and the Future of Mankind* (Kolkata: Advaita Ashrama, 2005), pp.80-1.

note what he wants to say. He made a scrutiny of different groups based upon qualities governing the societies. A society is a mixture of all such groups, with one group predominating others at a given time. Regarding the division in society, his views are in consonance with the classification of society into four classes of *Brahmins, Kshatriyas, Vaisyas* and *Sudras* on the wonderful scheme of *Varnasrama dharma* actuated and guided by the four *purusharthas*. Each individual has his own allotted duty according to his *varna* and *asrama*, hence it gives more stress on obligations rather than on rights and privileges. [52] He was also inspired by the ideal of social harmony and synthesis embodied in the theory of *Varnasrama* system. As it was chiefly intented to aid man in his evolution from biological to the spiritual plane of existence, he wished to retain the system with occasional readjustments.

Concept of Society-Harmony of the One and the Many

Society is viewed as an organic union of which each component forms an integral part of the society. In accordance with the Vedantic concept, society is composed of individuals who are spiritual in character. Hence society too, for Vivekananda is a divine institution and any change in society must have its base on spirituality. Since India is a spiritually oriented country, it was necessary for Vivekananda to develop a spiritual system of ideas, norms and values that would bring about a modification in the thought consciousness of the people and consequently advancement in society. Hence he is against the violent break with the

---

[52] D.R.Jatava, *op.cit.*, p.207.

Indian spiritual tradition. For him social change should be the outcome of the process of adjustment of old institutions and values to the new conditions.

The society which Vivekananda envisages correspond to the *Sahasrasirsa Purusa* (Universal/cosmic personality) which finds its reference in the Purusa-sukta in Rg-Veda.[53] There society with its four-fold divisions is viewed as a Cosmic Purusa, thousand headed, thousand-eyed and thousand-legged person who spreads over all the earth and rules over all living creatures.[54] It was stated that each class had originated from different parts of the cosmic person: the *Brahmin* from his mouth, *Kshatriyas* from his arms, and the *Vaisyas* from his thigh and *Sudras* from legs and that they act as an organic unity in order to maintain the cosmic order. The organic union with its many different components and all are essentially complete while preserving the diversity. It shows that the society functions as a well co ordinate single unit; in it none is inferior to the other. All are equally important and cooperative action of all these components are essential for the proper functioning of society. Each individual member of society must fulfill a certain function in it, thus contributing to the general welfare of the social structure as a whole. Vivekananda maintains that each component forms an integral part of the society and in the absence of one, the society fails to exist and function. By fulfilling the demands of both the inner and the outer

---

[53] M.N.Srinivas, Social Change in Modern India (NewDelhi: Orient Blackswan Pvt. Ltd., 2009), p.29.

[54] Swami Gautamananda, "Swami Vivekananda's Discoveries about India", PrabuddhaBharata, 82(1977), pp.13-14.

life of the individual, it aimed at social progress. He is in favour of *varna* classification in society as it is the stepping stone to civilization.

Diversity as an Essential Aspect of Society

Vivekananda realized that the abolition of the classification would lead to a dead uniformity of the society. He regards this diversity as an essential aspect for the community to survive. The evolution of the society is possible only by diversity[55]. In his opinion even though essentially same in accordance with the Vedantic precepts, no men and women in any society are of the same mind or capacity to do things. As unity in variety is the plan of all creation[56]. Thus he trusted in human inequality on the basis samkhya analysis of human nature and with the *Karma* theory emaciated in the Gita. Parallel to his affirmation of inequality as non eternal in accordance with the Advaita theory, is his explanation on the difference in creation with the doctrine of *gunas* in the samkhya theory. Diversity is not false by nature; however it becomes false when divorced from the unity which is the central truth. In this relation one would recall a verse in the Isopanisad which has its purport thus "... those who are devoted entirely to the principle of multiplicity and ignore the underlying unity enters into a blind darkness of ignorance. But those who are devoted entirely to the principle of indiscriminate unity ignoring the multiplicity enter into greater darkness because

---

[55] R.K.Dasgupta, ed., *Swami Vivekananda: A hundred years since Chicago* (Calcutta: Ramakrishna Mission 1994), p.333.

[56] *The Complete Works of Swami Vivekananda*, Vol.1, p.41.

such unity is reduced to blank identity or void."[57] Hence he regards diversity as the vital aspect of any society.

Advocate of Caste Mobility

Vivekananda made a striking analysis of different groups based upon the gunas governing the societies. It is these qualities of *sattva* (goodness), *Rajas* (egoism) and *tamas* (inertness) that constitute human personality. The difference in human qualities is due to the difference is degrees of interaction of these three *gunas*. Vivekananda argued that one or the other of these *gunas* in varying proposition will be inherent in every individual. The different classifications on the society as *Brahmin* (scholar), *Kshatriya* (warrior), *Vaisya* (tradesman), *sudra* (worker) is due to the difference in the degree of manifestation of qualities which are inherent in each man.[58] While emphasising the diversity, Vivekananda upholds the possibility to develop into a single community. A *Sudra* can become a Brahmin if he gains knowledge knowledge and imparts it to other. He proved that it is a quite possible for one to be changed from one caste into another by citing examples from Puranas of Viswamitra and Parasurama, who became Brahmana and Kshatriya respectively".[59] Hence Vivekananda upholds the possibility of caste mobility. While preserving the diversity in his concept of society, Vivekananda managed to develop a kind of single

---

[57] Amiya Kumar Mazumdar, *Rediscovering Vivekananda* (Kolkata: Advaita Ashrama, 2007), p.100.

[58] *The Complete Works of Swami Vivekananda*, Vol.4, p.449.

[59] *The Complete Works of Swami Vivekananda*, Vol.5, p.377.

community. Society is viewed as an organic union of which each component forms an integral part of the society. However according to him what made a man superior is not his caste but his inherent quality. With the Samkhya theory of gunas he explains that the qualities which make a man *Brahmin, Kshatriya, Vaisya* or *Sudra* depends on the predominance of *sattva, rajas* and *tamas*.[60] What Vivekananda wants to convey here is that each person is responsible for what he is. Accordingly it is these qualities which make one person a teacher, an administrator, a business man or a worker in a society. As the qualities in man do not stand fixed, there persist with him the chances for improvement and integration of his personality.

Caste, though accepted and appreciated by Vivekananda is not viewed as an achievement by *karma* and not a gift of birth. One's *karma* or action is his previous births determine the distribution of *gunas*. For him, the concept of *karma* which forms an essential part of Hindu thought, determines what we deserve and what can acquire.[61] Our present state is the result of what we thought and did in the past and our future depends on what we think and do now[62]. Here it follows that everyone is responsible for what he is. One could change his caste by acquiring the necessary qualities through the performance of *karma*. Quality is the criterion to determine one's caste. May be, this is the reason why he avers that "birth is nothing, the

---

[60] V. Sukumaran Nair, *Swami Vivekananda- The Educator* (NewDelhi: Sterling Publishers Pvt. Ltd., 1987), p.28.

[61] *The Complete Works of Swami Vivekananda*, Vol.1, p.31.

[62] Gautam Sen, *The Mind of Swami Vivekananda* (Mumbai: Jaico Publishing House, 2011), p.78.

environment is everything". [63] When one engages oneself in serving another for pay, he pitches himself in *shudrahood*, when one fights for what is right and just, then the qualities of *kshatriya* is reflected in him and one becomes a *brahmin* when he is engaged in meditation.[64] When one engages oneself in another for pay or busy transacting some piece for profit, he pitches himself in *sudrahood* and *vaisyahood* respectively. Here he intended to convey the message that any work done without expecting anything in return elevates that person to *brahminhood*.

Vivekananda states that any work done with a master's mind puts one really in a high position in the society. This is evident from the story of *'vyadha'* which he delivered in one of his lectures in Karma Yoga. The story described the importance of performance of *swadharma*. Any work done in sincerity and detachment can make one illumined. Vivekananda teaches that no duty is ugly or impure and it is the circumstances that make one perform a particular job. Each has his own position, but can reach the highest stage by expertise in such profession by the right performance of his duty selflessly. On the basis of views of Vivekananda, the highest culture resides in the conception of ideal *Brahminhood*. In this connection he also writes that *Brahminhood* cannot be associated with exclusive privilege of a few. He states that it is not the birth but the sincere action based on duty that makes one a *Brahmin*. In the Varna system, a Brahmin gets respect if he has acquired knowledge and imparts it to other. Thus he supported the old Indian institution of the four castes and four stages of

---

[63] *The Complete Works of Swami Vivekananda*, Vol.5, p.377.
[64] *idem*.

life that helps to attain a higher status. In the Varna system, a Brahmin gets respect if he has acquired knowledge and imparts it to other. Thus he supports the system which confers man a higher position on the ground that whether he had acquired knowledge and proficiency in his own profession and performs his work with utmost selflessness and sincerity.

Caste was a form of social organization and should be kept separate from religion. He opened that social organizations should change with the changing times. He asserted that as the caste in India has its base lying in spirituality, it is better than the caste which prevails in other Western countries.[65] In every other country the highest honour belongs to the *Kshatriyas*, the man of sword and wealth; but the ideal man according to Indian tradition is *Brahmin* – a man of spiritual culture and renunciation.[66] A caste of purity and self-sacrifice is better than a caste of dollars and power is what Vivekananda said to the western audience. Ideal of caste is meant for raising the entire humanity towards the realization of the great ideal of a spiritual man. He exhorted everyone in his country including the one belonging to the lower castes to bring out their very best, do *nishkamakarma* and try to become Brahmins".[67] So he did not want any leveling of caste rather proposed the raising up of the so called lower classes to the level of the higher.

---

[65] *ibid.*, p.214.

[66] *The Complete Works of Swami Vivekananda*, Vol.4, p.297.

[67] *The Complete Works of Swami Vivekananda*, Vol.5, p.49.

According to him caste system should be ennobled. It must be of the original caste system of the Vedic period which is free from the ugly and inhuman features of degrading the dignity of people on the basis of birth as the criterion of the caste and restricting certain realms of operation for a particular caste. But the scheme later deteriorated into an obnoxious one because of the claim of superiority and privileges by certain sections of the society on the basis of birth. *Varna* system exercised in ancient India differs much from the casteism based upon heredity. *Jati* system with its social and religious exclusivity should be overcome and caste is a means to help everybody in attaining the status of a true Brahmin, by being spiritually enlightened. This amounts to state that from caste we must reach a point when there is no caste at all[68]. Thus he advocated the concept of spiritual equality or democratic spiritualism.

Vivekananda put his finger on the evils of modern perverted caste system that kept the downtrodden masses away from the mainstream of the society. It is true that he had no repugnance towards the caste system of ancient society as he considered it as the natural order of any society. Vivekananda wanted everyone to have a thorough reading of scriptures in order to understand what the caste really indicates. He tried to bring back the true *Jati-dharma* which he thought a boon to the country[69] For him whatever nature gathers and provides us concentration of power, wisdom, and wealth as such is not necessarily an evil in fact, but he realized that these are all for diffusion whenever needed. We suffer because we ignore this noble truth. If they are left

---

[68] *ibid.*, p.214.

[69] *The Complete Works of Swami Vivekananda*, Vol.5, p.456-7

concentrated in the hand of a few, they become a social evil. Thus he strictly objected privileges and prejudices the caste system had brought in. The caste system in the modern period as a hindrance to the progress of Indian society as it kept the downtrodden masses away from the main stream of society. Vivekananda objected this kind of ill treatment of the people of the lower strata in the name of caste and custom. By depicting casteism and untouchability as an orthodox superstition and as a type of mental disease of the upper classes he tried to express his regret in a severe manner. Thus Vivekananda maintained that caste meant the raising of individuals towards the realization of the noble ideal of enlightened man.

Analyzing the historical facts available he comes to the conclusion that four fundamental social forces are ruling societies in the world. Indian history represented the principle of spiritualism, the history of Roman imperialism represented military action, the British mercantile aristocracy is the characteristics of the *Vaisyas* and the American democracy represented the sudrocracy.[70] Indians when ruled by the British *Vaisyas* become *Sudras*, independently of their former caste status. *Brahmins* and *kshatriyas* will rule within their respective nations whereas *Vaishya* rule has become international. He described the ruling *Vaishya* as those by whose command, the electricity carries messages in an instant from one place to another, by whose highway is the vast ocean with its mountain-high waves and at whose instance, commodities are being carried with the greatest ease from one part of the globe to another.[71]

---

[70] D.R.Jatava, *op.cit.*, p.206.

[71] *The Complete Works of Swami Vivekananda*, Vol.4, p.451.

During different regimes of different castes, society gained may things, both good and bad. Even though *Brahmin* rule promoted knowledge, its access was confined to a privileged section determined by birth.[72] *Kshatriya* rule was not as exclusive as the rule of *Brahmin*, but its demerit is in its cruel and tyrannical approach though it promotes art and culture.[73] Though Vivekananda criticized "The silent crushing and blood sucking, power, he appreciated the distributive spirit of *Vaisya* rule as they promoted spread the knowledge which was centralized during the previous two periods." [74] The wisdom and civilization and art that accumulated in the society during the *Brahmin* and *Kshatriya* supremacies are being diffused in all directions by the *Vaisyas* through their commerce. History shows that *sudras* were condemned in society in different periods. The advantage of the labourer rule will be the distribution of physical comforts; however there is the lowering of culture.[75] Despite the fact that there will be great distribution of ordinary education, promotion of extra ordinary geniuses will dwindle throughout the rule of *Vaisyas* and *sudras*. Vivekananda arrives at a conception of an ideal state in which the knowledge of the priest period, the culture of the military, and the distributive spirit of the commercial community and the deep sense of equality of the labourer can all be combined while minimizing their evils.[76] In the absence of such combination it would be difficult to

---

[72] *idem.*

[73] *The Complete Works of Swami Vivekananda*, Vol.6, p.381.

[74] *idem.*

[75] *idem.*

[76] Santi Nath Chattopadhyay, *op.cit.*, p.161.

create a harmonious as well as a vigorous and vibrant social order. But Vivekananda as a realist was not certain that human society can achieve such perfection at any point of time.

Vivekananda also favours the Hindu Social organization such as the four stages of life (*ashramas*) namely that of the student, the householder; the hermit and the monk.[77] Renunciation forms the basis of all these stages of life and it pervades the activities of all these stages of life. However in the last stage, man is required to renounce the world totally to gain spiritual wisdom. Those who cannot follow the path of total renunciation can adopt the path of action. If pursued with the spirit of yoga, both the paths prove equally effective for the individual to attain immortality. Vivekananda held that the life of action based on devotion and discrimination is as sacred as the path of renunciation.

Vivekananda was not against expertise of a profession linked with a particular group[78]. While he held that there exist differences of abilities, some people can do certain profession and occupations with more perfection than others[79]. But that is no reason for regarding one as superior to the other. The following words of Vivekananda bring to light this point clearly: "I can perform one duty in social life and you another, you can govern a country and I can mend why you are greater than I, for can you mend my shoes. Can I govern the country? I am clever in mending shoes.

---

[77] *The Complete Works of Swami Vivekananda*, Vol.1, p.42.

[78] William Radice, *op.cit.*, p.269.

[79] *idem*.

You are clever in reading Vedas, that is no reason why you should trample on my head..."[80]. The welfare of the society being the goal of social institutions, the *Varnasrama* system in one form or another will remain so long as nature has been skillful in providing a variation in the individual equipment by furnishing different aptitude for its maintenance. The soundness of the *Varnasrama system* is found in its hereditary character though it can be reckoned now as a drawback. But every social institution has its good points as well as bad point. In accordance with the *Varnasrama* system even the so called lowest person has a place in the society; it provides him the opportunities for improvement. Every individual had an equal position in the society like the smallest screw in a huge machine and the society worked smoothly and silently without any noise or murmur[81].

Vivekananda did not favour leaving the hereditary profession either.[82] While answering a question on this context, he opined that even with the awakening of knowledge, the potter can remain a potter, the fisherman, a fisherman, the peasant, a peasant. There is no need for them to leave their hereditary calling. There is no need to abandon the work in which one is born. Rather they should apply their knowledge to the better performance of the work to which they have been born. Such a situation, observed Vivekananda, will produce a good number of geniuses from

---

[80] Swami Vivekananda, *Lectures from Columbo to Almora* (Calcutta: Advaita Ashrama, n.d.), p.161.

[81] Eknath Ranade, *op.cit.*, p.46.

[82] Ajeet Jawed, *Swami Vivekananda: An Iconoclastic Ascetic* (New Delhi : Ane Books India, 2007), p.35.

among them in course of time.[83] Thus he explicitly reveals his liking for the hereditary profession and original caste system, based on one's capabilities.

However, Vivekananda turned his attention to the issues of modern perverted caste system in which he formed the practice of untouchability. He was opposed to such anti-social belief and held that modern casteism as a hindrance to national growth. The present caste is not the real *Jati*, but a hindrance to its progress. He held that "the caste had become a monstrous degradation, the opposite of what it was meant to be".[84] The main problem of caste is the practice of untouchability in which one person treats another as unclean. Even though he supported the tradition caste system, he was not a casteist. By supporting casteism, it means that one is willfully justifying an inhuman practice. Vivekananda holds that in accordance with one's capabilities one can live in any caste he would like. But that should not be the reason for his hatred towards another man or another caste. Vivekananda always stood for love among various sections of people"[85] and was very critical of social discrimination prevalent in Hindu society in the name of caste. Caste practice in the name of pollution or untouchability he called "diabolical old barbarianism".[86] He viewed untouchability as the worst social evil in India. Criticizing his co-religionists for the humiliations a low caste had to face and hypocrisy on the part of the higher

---

[83] *The Complete Works of Swami Vvekananda*, Vol.7, p.150.

[84] Jawaharlal Nehru, *The Discovery of India* (New Delhi: Oxford University Press, 1999), p.337.

[85] Swami Vivekananda, *To the youth of India*, p.50.

[86] *The Complete works of Swami Vivekananda*, p.50.

castes, he remarked, "Was there ever a sillier thing before in the world than what I saw in Malabar country? The poor pariah was not allowed to pass through the same street as the high caste man, but if he changes his name to a hodge-podge English name, it is a right, or to Mohammed as name, it is alright. What inference would you draw except that these Malabaris are all lunatics".[87] Thus he warned that if untouchability continues for another century, everyone in the country will be in a lunatic system.

Vivekananda also condemned the brahminical doctrine of *adhikaravada* which excluded the *sudras* from possessing the Vedic knowledge and from attaining power and wealth. It was a plea for social aristocracy.[88] He viewed *adhikaravada* as an outcome of selfishness because of its adherence to undemocratic dogma of rights and privileges of higher castes by curtailing the genuine rights of the *sudras*.[89] The forgoing analysis suggests that Vivekananda did not try to abolish the original caste system as several modern reformers did. He held that caste which was necessary and desirable in its early forms is meant to develop individuality and freedom.[90] But he tried to annihilate several evil practices in the name of caste and wanted to abolish its degenerated form. Complete equilibrium, he held, is never attained and would be fatal if it were attained; it would mean stagnation, atrophy and death. Even

---

[87] *ibid.*, pp.294-5.

[88] D.R.Jatava, *op.cit.*, p.207.

[89] *The Complete Works of Swami Vivekananda*, Vol.5, p.263.

[90] Jawaharlal Nehru, *op.cit.*, p.337.

commonest and oldest type of social classification is expressed as a dichotomy.[91] Its various forms distinguish the few and the many, the rich and the poor, the rulers and the ruled, and so on. The abolition of caste system would result in the creation of a new caste. In fact that was what happened to the AryaSamaj, BrahmaSamaj, the Lingayats of South India and the Sikhs of the Punjab.[92] Vivekananda brings our attention to the socio religious revolutions of the Buddha and Raja Ram Mohan Roy, who tried to pull down religion and caste altogether and failed.[93]

Vivekananda realized that the conception of caste was present in every society of the world. But he did not approve that system which is inconsistent with the democratic ideal of equal opportunities of life, liberty and pursuit of happiness. He realized that the solution of caste question lies not in the degradation of those who are already high up, but it comes by everyone fulfilling the dictates of the Vedantic religion by becoming illumined. In accordance with the scriptures it is states that everyone must make progress without stopping and that from the lowest man to the highest one. He advised the Brahmins to manifest the spirituality by discharging their responsibility of raising others to their status. This in many ways had led Ram Manohar Lohia to say later. He understood the caste system to be one of the greatest social systems possible, but , to put it in his own words, he also believed that, "…the unavoidable defects, foreign persecution and above all , the monumental ignorance

---

[91] Swami Suddhidananda, ed., *Vivekananda as the Turning Point* (Kolkata: Advaita Ashrama, 2013), p.257.

[92] Athalya. D.V., *Neo-Hinduism* (New Delhi: Ashish Publishing House, n.d.) p.185.

[93] *The Complete Works of Swam Vivekananda*, Vol.5, p.22.

and pride of many Brahmins who do not deserve the name, have thwarted, in many ways, the legitimate fructification of this most glorious Indian institution..."[94] In fact Vivekananda was of the opinion that the institution of caste was the most effective tool which keeps Indians away from all sorts of social inequalities as it objectives rest in the upliftment of every person to a status of the enlightened one. Hence he did not recommend the total abolition of caste as he considers it as a natural order for the progression of man. A major advantage of a spiritually oriented society (compared to a political or power dominated society) is the greater emphasis on selflessness, continence, hard work, self-control and renunciation. The essential things can be imbibed only by changing our outlook. And this change in outlook can only be achieved through the Vedantic ideal of oneness of mankind. It is by knowing that I and my brother as same, one can love and serve unselfishly and disinterestedly. While advising the Brahmins to manifest their divinity by raising others, what Vivekananda intends is that, it is only by selfless service that their divinity gets manifested. Thus he placed spiritual solidarity as the base for the social egalitarianism and well-being of the society.

Privilege as a bane to society

Vivekananda visualizes the idea of privilege as a curse to society as they form hindrance to social equality. In a lecture delivered in London on 'Vedanta and Privilege', Vivekananda spoke out against the phenomenon of privilege at all grades of society. He defined the concept of privilege as the enjoyment of advantages taken

---

[94] *The Complete Works of Swami Vivekananda*, Vol.7, p.214.

by one caste over another[95]. He held the view that one man born superior to another has no meaning according to Vedanta since all are equal and are manifestation of God. He therefore repudiates every privilege claimed by certain persons or classes of people. Vivekananda further mentioned about different types of privileges in the society such as the privilege of the strong over the weak, the rich over the poor, privilege of the intellect, privilege of spirituality.[96] While analysing different kinds of privileges, he realised that the worst one and most tyrannical is the privilege of spirituality because of their claim to know more of spirituality and of God. He ridiculed those people who considered themselves the messengers of God, the forerunners of spirituality and demanded worship and superior privileges in society[97]. Knowledge of God and of spirituality does not entitle anyone of greater privileges in society. But Vivekananda holds that those who demand any such privileges can neither be a Vedantist nor an illumined person, as he could not realise the God that exists in every human souls. Moreover, Vedanta claims that all knowledge is in every soul, even in the most ignorant, though he might not have manifested it because of his unfavourable circumstances. Having knowledge about the same, the idea that one man is born superior to the other has no place in the thought of Vivekananda

The false pride of birth on which the claim of superiority was based, is taken by Vivekananda as a sign of death and stagnation[98]. He states that one who is not

---

[95] *The Complete Works of Swami Vivekananda*, Vol.1, p.429.

[96] Amiya Kumar Mazumdar, *op.cit.,* p.155.

[97] *The Complete Works of Swam Vivekanada*, Vol.1, p.423

[98] *The Complete Works of* Swami Vivekanada, Vol. 4, p.300.

ready to give liberty to others does not deserve liberty for themselves[99]. He even suggested to the Brahmins that they should, like a cobra, suck the poison they had injected into the social body, in order to cure it, failure of which would lead to disastrous consequences[100]. He held the view that one should pray for oneself in order to realize God and there is no need for a priest or any other middle man in between[101]. Thus, as a sociologist and a realist, he raises his voice against priest-craft and the claim of superiority of Brahmins, through many of his writings and lectures.

By strongly opposing the privileges of any kind to any one section or class of people, Vivekananda stood for equality and freedom for all in the society. His concept of equality which was discussed stems from the Vedantic doctrine that the same spirit indwells in all beings[102]. When man realizes his 'oneness' with God, equality and freedom follows. Absolute equality or the perfect balance of all the struggling forces, in all the planes, says Vivekananda can never be attained in earthly life. Explaining the position of Vivekananda, B.N.Dutta writes: "He showed that no man is inferior to the other, no class has got special qualification than the other".[103] The Vedantic spirit of oneness makes the individual identify himself with the community and serves it with a service motive, without any personal gain. The

---

[99] *The Complete Works of Swam Vivekanada*, p.368.

[100] Ajeet Jawed, *op.cit.*, p.34.

[101] V. SukumaranNair, *Swami Vivekananda, The Educator* (New Delhi: Sterling Publishers Pvt. Ltd., 1987), pp. 80-1.

[102] *ibid.*, p.125.

[103] BhupendranathDutta, *Swami Vivekananda: Patriot Prophet* (Calcutta: Nava Bharath Publication, 1954), p.327.

individual's life is in the life of the whole and the individual's happiness is in the happiness of the whole. Apart from the whole, the individual existence is inconceivable- this is an eternal truth and is the bed-rock on which the universe is built.[104] The happiness and welfare of all has its base on the concept of equality of all. He wanted to revive society upon the old grounds of universal salvation and equality, as laid down in the thoughts of Sankara, Ramanuja and the like. But in spite of the teachings of these old masters ancient Indians did not try to give a practical expression to these metaphysical ideals of equality[105]. Vivekananda affirms that it was Sri Ramakrishna, who for the first time has become conscious of affinity of Vedanta with the doctrine of human equality and its practical application. Regarding this he avers: "We may see many persons talking fine things about charity, about equality and the rights of other people and all that, but it was only in theory. I was so fortunate as to find one who was able to carry theory into practice. He had the most wonderful facilities of carrying everything into practice which he thought was right".[106] In his lectures on 'Practical Vedanta', Vivekananda has shown how the theoretical side is to be supplemented with the practical side. So that unity can be realized in this life itself. He held that the Vedanta can provide all the modern equalizing theories with a spiritual basis[107].

---

[104] *The Complete Works of Swami Vivekananda*, Vol .4, p.463.

[105] S.L.Malhotra, Social and Political Orientation of Neo-Vedanta (New Delhi: S.Chand and Co.,1970), p.115.

[106] *The Complete Works of Swami Vivekananda*, Vol.4, p.174.

[107] *The Complete Works of Swami Vivekananda*, Vol.5, pp.212-3.

Equality of Opportunity

Vivekananda favours the modern principle of equality of opportunity. The principle of equality reveals that each individual has the same right and full opportunity to develop his mental ability. It indicates that our social and economic arrangements should never hamper the natural endowments of others. If same opportunity is made open to all, those who are physically capable and mentally alert will take advantage of it, where as those who are physically and mentally deficient may fail to take advantage of the same. Moreover, Vivekananda while advocating equality of opportunity, realized that the weaker ones in the society, the poor and the down trodden should be provided with additional opportunities for the development of their inmate faculties. As he says: The weaker should be given more chance than the strong in the society.[108] Later Gandhiji also adopted the same stand when he advocates the doctrine of equal distribution. This concept of equality and freedom, Vivekananda holds form the main content in the development of an egalitarian society.

He gave importance to the laboring masses and considered them as the backbone of any nation.[109] If these labouring classes such as the sweepers and the farmers stop working, our society will come to a standstill.[110] He considered the

---

[108] Kalpana Mohapatra, *Political Philosophy of Swami Vivekananda* (NewDelhi: Northern Book Centre,1996), p.67.

[109] *The Complete Works of Swami Vivekananda*, Vol.7, p.346.

[110] *idem.*

wealthy to be dead rather than alive, and thought they should not be trusted. The neglect of the masses is the main cause for the deficiency of Indian society. His consideration for the laboring masses of our country is evident when he says "The whole defect is here: The real nation who lives in cottage has forgotten their manhood, their individuality.[111]

Cultural Upheaval of the Masses

Culture, which comprises one of the principal elements of preparation of life in society, plays a meticulous role in its development. Culture does not mean the forms of adoption or the forms of marriage, but they are the fundamental basic verities which are permanent, ceaseless and cannot be superseded by any kind of advances which science or history may make.[112] Each nation and each separate civilization finds development in its own culture that had its roots in generations hundreds and thousands of years ago. This is same in the case of individuals also. The inner growth of a man, the way he behaves to others, his capacity to understand the other person, all these comprise his culture. It is through Sanskrit language, the great classics of India or the above mentioned fundamental basic truths could be fully grasped with all its relevance. Being the treasure house of ancient wisdom the study of the Classics can lead to cultural upheaval amongst the downtrodden masses who are placed in a

---

[111] *TheComplete Works of Swami Vivekananda*, Vol.8, p.307.

[112] *President Radhakrishnan's Speeches and Writings* (New Delhi: Director, Publication Division, Patalia House, 1969), p.228.

very low esteem in the society. It might be because of this reason, Vivekananda suggested broadening the access of Sanskrit education and through it the great classics of the nation should be broadcast and made known to all sections of the society. Society based on wisdom will diminish the distinctions and will increase the capacity to work together. It has relevance even in the present day society as culture accelerates man's capacity to work together, making them creative, innovative, open to change capable of building permanent social bonds preventing exclusion and social pathologies thereby promotes social integration.

Democratization of Education

Vivekananda's ideas on education have a democratic angle as well. The monopolizing of the whole education of the land among a handful of men, he observed, is the cause of India's ruin.[113] A nation is advanced in proposition only as education and intelligence spread among the masses. He takes mass education as an instrument to improve the individual as well as society. He exhorted: "No amount of politics would be of any avail until the masses of Indian are once more well-educated, well- fed and well-cared for."[114] In the matter of mass education he differ from Plato who made no provision for the education of the lowest classes.[115] Plato stressed the development of the individuality of the rulers, who was the guide of the masses. But

---

[113] A. R. Mohapatra, *Social Philosophy of Swami Vivekananda* (New Delhi: Read worthy Publication (P)Ltd., 2009), p.54.

[114] M. H. Siddique, *Philosophical and Sociological Perpectives in Education* (New Delhi: APH Publishing Corporation, 2009), p.74.

[115] C.L. Wayper. *Political Thought* (Bombay: B J Publications, 1979), p.30.

in modern age, the education and civilization penetrated into the masses of the West at large. This was considered as the reason for their prosperity according to Vivekananda.

Vivekananda envisaged the modern idea about social education. He says: "If the poor boy cannot come to education, education must go to him."[116] He wanted the self-sacrificing *sannyasins* in India to organize them to teach the villagers secular things rather than preaching religion. Education alone will help the poor to acquire faith in their own selves and thereby will have self-awareness and self-confidence. It helps develops their lost individuality which is not in the body but in the soul of man. In short, the social relevance of Vivekananda's educational ideas lies in emphasis on integrated development of the human personality in the ascending scale of body, mind and heart, cultivation of fearlessness in pursuit of truth, compassion and fraternity in dealing with fellowmen, upliftment of women and the common man and the absorption of the spirited message of Vedanta tilt all men are divine.

Demerits of Indian Educational System

Vivekananda was critical of educational system of his time which is totally intellectualized with least place for the expansion of heart. He observes that the Indian education system does not produce a man of originality; On the other hand the system destroys one's faith and self-confidence. Quoting his own words "The child is taken

---

[116] J. C. Aggarwal, *Theory and principles of education* (New Delhi: Vikas Publishing House Pvt. Ltd., 2004), p.209.

to school, and the first thing he learns is that his father is a fool, the second that his grandfather is a lunatic, the third thing that all his teachers are hypocrites, the fourth that all sacred books are lies ! By the time he is sixteen he has a mass of negation, lifeless and boneless. As the result is that fifty years of such education has not produced one original man in the three Presidencies".[117] Hence he was highly critical of the then existing educational system which lacks attention to the development of the mental ability and moral character in its pupils. He wanted a through re-orientation of the educational system.

Man-making Education

Through education, Vivekananda wants to create a new class of people who can lead cooperative and mutually helpful living. They must be trained to develop empathy rather than intellectual abilities. He had taught that acquisition of knowledge and skill, but also to help one to live with others. Education must harmonize and develops his physical, mental, intellectual and spiritual faculties and prepares him for complete living. Education is not to be considered as information that is put into the brain of the student. He says that if education is identical with information, the libraries are the greatest sages in the world and encyclopedias the Rishis[118]. The aim of education must rather be assimilation of ideas. He views that "If a person has assimilated five ideas and made them part of his life and character, he acquires more

---

[117] *The Complete Works of Swami Vivekananda*, Vol.3, p.302.

[118] J.C.Aggarwal, *op.cit.*,p.206.

education than any man who has got by heart a whole library[119]. He scoffed at the importance being given to book learning and memory training. Education that is totally intellectualized with no place given for the expansion of the heart or ennobling individual's nature may detriment him from his social responsibilities by strengthening his selfish tendencies. Moral qualities are of greater value than intellectual accomplishment. In the opinion of Sri Ramakrishna knowledge which purifies the mind and heart and raises the man to an elevated level, is true knowledge. Following his master, Vivekananda holds that education should cultivate capabilities to work and sensibility to feel the joy and sorrow of others.

The salutary effect of all education, according to Vivekananda should be man making, life giving and character building. The end and the aim of all training are to make the man grow towards his natural end. The goal of true education is reached only by which the expression of will is brought under control. The method prescribed for controlling the will is based on the concepts of Advaita and yoga. They work in union for the development of a balanced personality or a total man, a man fit to discharge his social obligations. The real aim of education Vivekananda held is self-realization which is similar to the Socratic dictum 'know thyself'. The essence of Vedanta which proclaims the divine nature of every soul must be ingrained in our education system. Education is manifestation of that divinity in man, one that helps to reach self-actualization. Vivekananda envisions that only by this process he would be

---

[119]*idem.*

equipped to live as a part of community.[120] A sustainable human development is possible only through the eternal teachings of Vedanta which ensures self-realisation and afterwards to break down the barriers class and privilege and makes him feel for the suffering of the poor.

Recognizing the significance of personal influence of the teacher in imparting education Vivekananda suggested the ancient *gurukula*[121] system whilst incorporating into itself all that is best and assimilable in occidental thought.[122] In such system, the student has close association with his teacher, right from the boyhood. A comprehensive and fruitful preparation for life as a whole can be accomplished by the careful attention of the teacher who is a man of character. In order to kindle the mind of the pupils with wisdom, teachers ought to know the spirit of the scriptures[123] and should possess certain ideal qualities. He should set an example for his pupils to follow in all the sphere of life. His objectives must not be money, name or fame. Any such selfish motives, he held will cause destruction to the conveying medium. S. Radhakrishnan and Dewey maintained the same view regarding the quality of a teacher. Only a man of character is capable of inculcating positive tendencies like self-realization in the mind of the taught. Hence he points out the importance of

---

[120] Padma Ramachandran and ValsaRavikumar, *Education in India* (New Delhi: National Book Trust), p.3.

[121] The system of education in which the student had to leave home at an early stage and live in teacher's house hold to study closely under his supervision till the completion of education is called *gurukula* system, by the historians.

[122] D. Vable, *The AryaSamaj*, p.114 citied in William Radice, ed., *op.cit.,* p.199.

[123] *The Complete Works of Swami Vivekananda*, Vol.3, p.58.

drawing a good proportion of the best personalities in the country into the teaching profession.

During their education in the *gurukula* system, the student must be completely obedient to their teachers and also, be celibate and exercise self-discipline. This is inconsonance with the noblest conception of Hindu social organization which speaks of the four fold stages in life, of which the first is *brahmacharya* or the student life. During this stage one should observe chastity in thought, word and deed. Vivekananda says that by observing *brahmacharya*, all learning can be mastered in a very short time and one could acquire unfailing memory of what one knows and learns[124]. He must be provided with an education which enables him to enhance his nature making him free from suspicion, jealousy and conceit and thereby make him cooperative and mutually helpful life. Here his educational view stands close to that of Bertrand Russell's who states its aim as developing minds sensitive enough to perceive and feel the shocks of tragedies taking place in societies. Students are guided to approach life's problem with fortitude, self-control and sense of balance which our present condition demanded. Without the cultivation of this disciplines, Vivekananda warns that the students become a danger to themselves and to the society.

According to Indian tradition the key to true knowledge can be obtained through concentration. In accordance with this Vivekananda also held that the very essence of education is concentration of mind. He says: "If I had to do my education

---

[124] *The Complete Works of Swami Vivekananda*, Vol .3, p.319.

over again, and had any voice in the matter, I would not study facts at all. I would develop the power of concentration and detach, and then with a perfect instrument, I could collect fact at will."[125] Thus training of the mind is very important for Vivekananda's scheme of education. Our mind may get concentrated on a subject which we are interested. But that is not real concentration because it must be an act of will. Real concentration needs training. Thus a trained mind gets focused on whatever objects it like. An untrained mind takes us astray while a trained mind leads us in the right path. It is the difference in the degrees of concentration that makes the man the highest and lowest. The more concentrated he is the better will be his thought and understanding. Both for acquiring secular and spiritual knowledge, concentration play an important role. He says, "In making money or in worshipping god, or in doing anything the stronger the powers of concentration, the better will that thing be done[126]. Thus the success in life mostly depends on the power of concentration. One should be like an oyster that patiently develops a drop of water into a pearl. What he meant probably is that first of all one has to hear, then understand, and then leaving all distractions, shutting the mind to outside influences and devote oneself to develop the truth within you[127]. He reminds here, of the danger of frittering away of energies by taking up an idea for its novelty, and then giving it up for another that is newer. When one takes up one idea, he should not give it up until he reaches his goal. So he

---

[125] *The Complete Works of Swami Vivekananda*, Vol.6, pp.38-9.

[126] *The Complete Works of Swami Vivekananda*, Vol.2, p.391.

[127] Swami Chetananda, ed., *Meditation and its Method* (Kolkata: Advaita Ashrama, 2008), p.53.

advises that in order to be a successful a person needs to take up an idea and makes that idea his life by constantly thinking about it and striving to achieve it.

Vivekananda was against all compulsion in teaching as it creates obstinacy and defiance. He wanted to abolish the system which aimed at training students in the manner as that of "the man who battered his ass, being advised that it could thereby be turned into a horse."[128] Education should be imparted to student in a natural way with love. The child should be taught through by love, it makes fellow feelings and love for human beings. He held that it is not good from the part of parents and teachers to constantly tax their children to read and write or to weaken their minds by calling them fools[129]. Constant encouragement and kind words imbibe positive thought in them on the contrary.

Vivekananda opined that education alone is capable to develop strength for the masses. The nature of strength according to him has double significance. He considers weakness as a sign of moral degeneration due to the lack of strength and faith in oneself. Weakness is the human inability to demonstrate God's nature, which ultimately leads to moral and social destruction. Vivekananda considers weakness as the cause of all miseries in the world. "We lie, steal, kill and commit other crime because we are weak."[130] Again he combined weakness with lack of social morality. Stating "We are lazy, we cannot work; we do not love each other, we are intensely

---

[128] *The Complete Works of Swami Vivekananda*, Vol.7, p.268.

[129] Eknath Ranade, *op.cit*, p.143.

[130] *The Complete Works of Swami Vivekananda*, Vol.2, p.198.

selfish" [131] because of our weakness. Truly speaking, weakness, for him, is the root causes of the destruction of social harmony which causes slavery and death. Weakness prevents one form seeing abilities hidden within oneself. Instead of finding our own potentialities we blame other for our fault and we are very slow to recognize our weakness.[132] Weakness prevents growth as well as social development.

To cure this imperfection of weakness one should have faith in oneself. He held. "The only cause is that you are weak, you have no faith in yourself".[133] It is the difference in *sraddha* (faith) that makes difference between man and man. He said that losing faith in one's self is same as losing faith in God. According to him a man who has no faith in himself could not attain salvation.

Women as the main component of Society

Vivekananda had a deep concern for women who were deprived of basic human rights though being an important component of the human society. Being the repository of the glorious qualities of chastity, purity and motherhood, she commanded worshipful attitude from men. He invites on attention to the Vedic age where woman enjoyed almost every privilege as men in the civic and religious sphere.[134] But in some later periods of Indian history, women were not treated with fairness and dignity. The dominant ideal however has been one of perfect equality. In

---

[131] *The Complete Works of Swami Vivekananda*, Vol.3 , p.241.

[132] *The Complete Works of Swami Vivekananda*, Vol.2, p.224.

[133] *idem.*

[134] *The Complete Works of Swami Vivekananda*, Vol.3, p.505.

the pursuit of knowledge and virtue and in the performance of rituals and of wars, the Vedic women were companions and helpmates of men. As quoted by S.Radhakrishnan from the Ramayana, King Janaka asked Rama to treat Sita as his companion of all duties, on the occasion of their marriage.[135] Vivekananda also found it extremely right to show no distinction between men and women, based on the Vedanta which declares that one and the same conscious self is present in all beings.[136] It is known to him that in the highest reality of Para Brahman, there exists no distinction of sex. Such distinction is being noticed only on the relative plane.[137] The difference between men and women is outward and he proclaims, "in their real nature there is none"[138] The aforesaid views picture Vivekananda as an advocate of gender equality.

Advocate of Gender Equality

In spite of the psychological and physiological difference basically he never accepted the inequality between the sexes: He believed that their roles are complementary. The real wellbeing of the society can be achieved only through their

---

[135] Robert A.Mc.Dermott, ed., *The Basic Writings of S.Radhakrishnan* (Mumbai: JaicoPublshing House, 2007), p.228.

[136] R.N.Sharma, *Contemporary Indian Philosophy* (NewDelhi: Atlantic Publishers and Distributors, 1991), p.56.

[137] *The Complete Works of Swami Vivekananda*, Vol.3, p.219.

[138] *idem.*

mutual cooperation based on cordiality and respect.[139] Men and women are equally good and important to the society. No man can bring up a child with as such patience, endurance and love as a woman. Vivekananda wanted to judge men and women by the standard of their respective greatness and he knew that a man or woman can never replace one another. [140] "Just as a bird cannot fly on a single wing, people cannot progress without uplifting its women folk" [141] Vivekananda had quoted. He considers men and the women as the two wheels of the society, without the effective working of the two, the society cannot make progress.[142] Family forms the miniature of society. There is no hope for rise for that family where there is no esteem for women and where they live in sadness. Quoting *Manusmrithi* he had spoken that where women are respected, the Gods delight and where they are not respected, all the efforts of a society come to a naught.[143] He accused Indian men for not respecting women, the real image of *Sakthi*, which was one of the reasons for India's degradation.

The status women enjoyed during the Vedic period gradually degenerated. During the age of the Vedas there were women who boldly renounced the shackles of

---

[139] Lekshmi.R, *Humanism of Vivekananda* (Thiruvananthapuram: Ramakrishna Sarada Mission, 2005), p.127.

[140] *The Complete Works of Swami Vivekananda*, Vol.2, p.26.

[141] Swami Suddhasatwananda, ed., *Thus spake Vivekananda* (Madras: Ramakrishna Matt, 1963), p.94.

[142] *The Complete Works of Swami Vivekananda*, Vol.2, p.283 .

[143] Swami Suddhidananda, ed., *op.cit.*, p.165.

familial bond to pursue their spiritual goals.[144] However, in the medieval period there was a degeneration of these ideals, obnoxious beliefs deteriorated the minds of our society and it came to be considered that women are unfit for the pursuit of knowledge and devotion. The degeneration that was seen in the status of women was owing to several social and political factors that occurred in the eighteenth and the nineteenth centuries. Child marriage, polygamy, sati, prohibition of widow remarriages, denial of right to education and a hoard of other disabilities imposed on the women folk had stifled the very source of well-being of Indian society. Vivekananda opposed all these evils. He characterized child marriage as a devilish custom, ridiculed such unscientific practices and castigated its supporters. He criticized the scriptures like *GrihyaSutra* and *Brahmanas* and their commentaries for supporting child marriage.[145]

Views Regarding the Institution of Marriage

Vivekananda had a very clear and definite idea regarding the institution of marriage. Marriage in the Indian context is not so simple, but it had a greater and deeper meaning. Marriage according to him is a matter of social institution than a matter concerning the individual alone. Accordingly decisions taken by the society were given more importance than that of its subjects. It is a partnership in which the husband and wife have their rights and discharge their respective obligations as well. He is in perfect agreement with the Indian conception that marriage is not for sensual

---

[144] Swami Suddhidananda, *op.cit.*, p.171.

[145] *The Complete Works of Swami Vivekananda*, Vol.4, p.477.

gratification, but for perpetuation of the human race. Regarding this he said: "Forget not that thy marriage, thy wealth, thy life are not for self-pleasure, are not for the individual personal happiness... thou are born as a sacrifice to the Mother's altar"...[146]

The state of the householder is the mainstay of social life. It is said that the householder shall have his life established in the supreme reality and shall dedicate to the Eternal Being whatever activities he undertakes. A similar view can be observed in the writings of S.Radhakrishnan when he says that man and woman are servants of a higher ideal to which their individual inclinations are to be subordinated.[147] Again, Vivekananda states that if individual pleasures or satisfaction of animal instincts were the criterion in selecting one's life partner, the result must be brutal children who will be responsible for the evil of the society.[148] He recalls the sayings of Manu that a child that is born of lust is not an Aryan.[149] Lesser the number of 'Aryan' children in a society greater the possibility of malevolence in the society. Regarding marriage, he held that the decision of society must be taken in to account. He advised that so long as one lives in a society, one must sacrifice one's personal desires for the public good.[150] This is in contradiction to the views held by Rabindranath Tagore, a champion of individual freedom, as he holds obedience to ecclesiastical pundits or

---

[146] *Vivekananda his Call to the Nation: A Compilation* (Kolkata: Advaita Ashram, 2005), p.94.

[147] Dr.S.Radhakrishnan, *The Hindu View of life* (1927, rpt., Bombay: George Allen and Unwin (India) Pvt., 1976), p.60.

[148] *The Complete Works of Swami Vivekananda*, Vol.3, p.408.

[149] Swami Vivekananda, *Education for character*, p.133.

[150] *The Complete Works of Swami Vivekananda*, Vol.3, p.408.

social rules in a form of self-indulgence, even as action in obedience to ones deepest being is the imperative command of life. In Tagore's view as beauty is higher than harmony, as truth is higher than consistency, so is love higher than law[151] and so he despises organization and believes in each man living his own life in his own way.

Again Vivekananda was against the irrationality of forbidding inter-caste marriage. Like the Brahma Samaj leaders, he suggested that inter marriages might break the compartmentalization in Indian society, drawing every one closer to each other. Moreover he held that in the absence of inter caste marriages in India; the race will become weaker and weaker.[152] So he wanted to root-out the tendency of keeping marriage relationships confined within the limited socio-cultural unit of society. He reprimanded marital alliance between cousins and near relations as it will physically deteriorate the race.[153] It might be because of the influence of Western scientific knowledge Vivekananda adopted such a stand. He advised his countrymen that, only by widening the circle of marriage it would be possible to infuse a new and a different kind of blood in to our progeny so that they may be saved from the clutches of many our present- day diseases and other consequent evils.[154] Regarding inter-provincial marriage, he did not ask for any radical transformation considering that it might take a very long period for such a progress in society.[155] It is clear that Vivekananda was not

---

[151] Robert A.McDermott,ed., *op.cit.,* p.253.

[152] *The Complete Works of Swami Vivekananda.,* Vol.5, p.334.

[153] *ibid.,* pp.340-1.

[154] *ibid.,* p.341.

[155] *ibid.,* p.340.

a social revolutionary, as he simply advocated a way of moderation in the process of social change.

In the case of widow remarriage, Vivekananda adopted a non-committal attitude. He held that as the problem dealt mostly with the grown up women, they could take apt decision if provided with proper education. He opined that the Catholics and the Hindus had kept marriage as sacred and inviolable; thereby they could produce many chaste men and women of immense power.[156] On another occasion he said that he could not find a nation whose fate was determined by the number of husbands their widows could get. [157] Hence the solution Vivekananda laid for the issue of widow re marriage was in the free choice to be taken by the educated women themselves.

Vivekananda regards that monastic life is possible for women also. While one of his disciples raised objection against this he had once said that Vedanta declares the same conscious self is present in all beings. He holds that those women who lead the monastic life can dedicate themselves for realizing the ideal of Indian womanhood.[158] Even while idolizes the concept of motherhood and traditional values of Indian women Vivekananda does not stand against any healthy outlook on the role of women in society, their rights and dignity. Vivekananda knew that the problems that Indian

---

[156] *The Complete Works of Swami Vivekananda*, Vol.5, p.180.

[157] *ibid.*, p.224.

[158] Nemai Sadhan Bose, *Makers of Indian Literature: Swami Vivekananda* (New Delhi: Sahitya akademi, 1997), pp.94-5.

women face can be traced to their attempt to jump out of the old spiritual inheritance. He said that the women of India should be built upon the ideal of Sita.[159] Trying to make women modern away from the mould of Sita has been the bane of our socio-cultural strivings. He wanted women to imbibe the power of tolerance and forbearance that Sita possessed. Referring to the Queen of Jhansi, he wanted women to acquire the spirit of valour and heroism and stressed on the necessity of learning the art of self-defence.[160]

Vivekananda made an analysis on the attitude of Indian men and their Western counter parts toward women and opined the Westerns as *Shakti* worshippers in the true sense of the term. Women were given a very high status in the West, hence he realised that their '*Sakthipooja*' is actual and not ritualistic as in India. He viewed, "Even in worship it is to Mary that prayers are mostly addressed among the catholic: 'Ave Maria' is the cry heard everywhere".[161] He added that the Women's state in the West is foremost and great personal attention is paid to her. As they were provided with good education, right and equal states as men, they contributed equally in the development of their respective countries. Vivekananda during his stay in America came to know that the women were not dependent upon the men folk for their survival.[162] They were not dominated by males and enjoyed freedom in every sphere. This made him raise voice against the poor condition of women in his own society.

---

[159] *The Complete Works of Swami Vivekananda*, Vol.4, pp.479-80.

[160] Swami Suddhidananda, *op.cit.*, p.97.

[161] *The Complete Works of Swami Vivekananda*, Vol.5, p.506.

[162] Ajeet Jawed, *op.cit.*, p.44.

He perceived that women in India have been trained in helplessness and servile dependence on others which was responsible for their low status in society. As women are the life and soul of every nation, he earnestly wanted that all learning and culture of a nation must be centered on them. He accused the men of his own country for treating women as 'despicable worms', 'gateway to hell' and so forth.[163]

Though he pleaded for women emancipation and empowerment, he did not want either Indian women to imitate Western women blindly or the women in the West to imitate Indian women in a blind way. By blindly imitating someone else one will never become the self that he or she should be. An ass in a lion's skin never becomes a lion said Vivekananda in this context and hence western culture should not be imitated.[164] Both the cultures have their own merit and demerit. Hence it is unfair to judge women in the East by the western standard and vice versa. He spoke for both the East and West and knew that each had something to contribute to the development of the other. If the west could profit by taking note of the Eastern ideal of womanhood, centering round Motherhood, the East also could profit by adopting the qualities like self-dependence, wide culture and other active virtues which the western women possessed.[165] That man or that society which has nothing to learn is already in the jaws of the death. There are many things to learn, we must struggle for new and higher things till we die. It may be said that the ideal of womanhood Vivekananda

---

[163] Letters dated 28 December 1893, *Swami Vivekananda Letters*, p.80 cited in Chaturvedi Badrinath, *op.cit.*, pp.191-2.

[164] *The Complete Works of Swami Vivekananda*, Vol.4, p.477

[165] *idem.*

expressed like any other idea is a unique synthesis of the past, present and future, the East and the West. He wanted the good, be it of the past or present, be it from of any other cultures, need to be accepted and assimilated to our culture. Thus Vivekananda was a man of enculturation.

Vivekananda suggested that there is no tool more effective than education to make women self-dependent and can put them in a position to solve their own problems. Along with bookish knowledge, girls should be taught History and the *Puranas*, house-keeping, the arts, the duties of home-life and the principles that help form an ideal character.[166] He held that worship and meditation should be given prime importance in their curriculum.[167] He said women must learn modern science, but not at the cost of the ancient spirituality. Along with bookish knowledge he recommended that girls should be taught housekeeping, duties of home life and principles that help form an ideal character, thereby they will be fit enough for taking the big responsibility of being a mother to perfection. He envisioned that only in the homes of educated and pious mother that the great men will be born. Vivekananda observes that sound education is essential for taking the big responsibilities of being a mother to perfection. Education which has its base on spirituality alone can help them become ideal matrons of home.[168] The children of such mothers, he said will be capable to make progress in virtues that distinguish the mothers. By stressing the need of good parentage, he firmly believed that only in the homes of an educated and pious mother

---

[166] Swami Vivekananda, *Education for character*, p.136.

[167] *Idem.*

[168] *The Complete Works of Swami Vivekananda*, Vol.6, p.489.

can great men take birth. Moral and spiritual children can be expected only when the parents are educated and good. Accordingly prenatal influences do give an impetus to the child in showing good or evil characters in the future.[169] It is the women who mould the next generation, hence the destiny of the country. Hence Vivekananda realised that there is nothing greater for social improvement than bringing up a healthy, intelligent and cultured generation which educated, pious mothers alone can provide.

Role of Youth in Social Service

Vivekananda inspired the youth of India through his speeches and writings on the ideas in social service and character building. He preached the Eastern ideal of renunciation and western concept of services simultaneously. He taught his disciples: "Our idea is to achieve salvation for individual and the welfare of the world. The greatest goal of life is self-emancipation. Thus he preached not only for man-making but also for world- moving. He wanted the resourceful youth of India to dedicate themselves for the services of their motherland. He called upon to devote themselves to the nation with worshipful endurance.

Though Vivekananda had advocated this type of patriotism in several places, he never participated in any political movements as he remained non-political and never apolitical. The inspiration which the young men like Alasinga and his fellow disciples

---

[169] *The Complete Works of Swami Vivekananda*, Vol.8, p.60.

received from Vivekananda was that of patriotism, but the patriotism that he imparts to them was not narrow in outlook as he upholds a mode of internationalism.

Vivekananda wanted the youth to be strong physically, mentally and spiritually and to be prepared for social action. The youth of the country need to act and not just talk to build up a strong nation and for this they need vigour in the blood and strength in the muscles. He held that neither speeches nor criticisms benefit the people and the existing social situation. A true reformer has to find out practical solutions to the problems instead of condemnation. Many people have talked about social reformations of ideals and other such things. The qualities which Vivekananda attributed to a true reformer are the same as the qualities of a self realized person inscribed in Indian tradition. Hence Vivekananda's views reveal the fact that a self realized person alone can be a true reformer.

Vivekananda observes the measure of advance and decline of a society by relating it to periods when it had its mind open or closed to the outside world .Vivekananda said · "My idea as to the key note of our national down fall is that we do not mix with other nations – that is the one and the sole cause[170]". Without dynamic outlook, there will be stagnation and decay. Many of the things which are valuable had been brought about because of the receptive attitude towards social change. However, if change occurs very rapidly it may create new problems for which we are unprepared. So instead of introducing a better society, it can give people a constant sense of uncertainty and insecurity Hence every social group feels

---

[170] *The Complete Works of Swami Vivekananda* ,Vol 5, p. 220

the need for some degree of stability. If this stability is maintained change must be gradual. That is the reason why Vivekananda says thus: "what I say is not 'Reform' but 'Move on'"[171]. There must be a balance struck between stability and change. From the resting ground of Indian traditions, he tried to embrace various thoughts which are alien to him. The aforesaid view is his ascertainment that change must take place by evolution rather than by revolution.

---

[171]*ibid.*, Vol. 6, p. 110

CHAPTER- V

CONCLUSION

Vivekananda is a great philosopher for his far reaching social ideals and humanistic concepts. He was aware of the fact that the genuine wisdom of Vedanta, being in its highest phase the fruit of a transcendental insight, is sublimely dateless and unchangeable. Yet its mode of expression is necessarily dated and therefore needs change. As his thought has its base on the ancient wisdom of India, he does not claim that an entirely new teaching has been given to the world. But by his teachings the speculative philosophical ideas of traditional Vedanta and Yoga which were held in a primitive antique form have been brought up-to-date and given a scientific modern expression. He has made it accessible to the common man in a simple yet in an authentic manner. Vivekananda holds that philosophy can never be placed under any abstract ideas unconnected with life's problems nor can it be considered as something which deals with theory only, forgetting the significance of the man and his life. As philosophy apprehends the whole of man, and not his conceptual thoughts, intellect, feelings, body or relation to the world around him, it cannot be confined to any abstract ideas. A balance and an attempt at harmony between these is what an authentic philosophy recommends. Vivekananda while saying thus: "The true philosophy should be the mother of spiritual action, the fountain-head of creative energy, and the highest and noblest stimulus to the will. Short of that it is worthless",[1] it is actually establishing the authenticity of his thought. He fulfilled this mission His neo-Vedanta is an attempt in converting the abstract thoughts of Advaita to living poetic in the everyday life of man. It has ever remained a philosophy of helping man to transcend the triviality of his daily life and to make his personal and social life authentic, purposeful and tending towards perfection.

Man being a social animal, it is only in espousal with the society that any ideal or thought regarding him can bear fruit. Hence a philosophy must deal with man's entire life, his contact with other people; the principles which guide him in dealing with them, his attitude towards himself and a lot more. Being so the function of a philosopher is not just to give a theory which has no relevance to social context, but to critically reflect over them and find ways for understanding the changing situations. Vivekananda as a true social philosopher, points out the mistake of confining the teachings of Vedanta to the spiritual realm or to the lives of the monks. He has made his thought down-to-earth and socially acceptable by freeing it from the subtleties of the traditional Vedanta. Instead of preaching other worldliness, it stands as an affirmation of life on earth and does not encourage indifference to social engagements. He has converted the abstract ideals of Vedanta, applied it in the

---

[1] Eastern and Western Disciples, *The Life Of Swami Vivekananda* (Kolkata: Advaita Ashrama, 2007),Vol.1, p.102.

context of family and social life, in an intelligible, concrete, scientific and practical manner to meet the demands of man and of the society as a whole.

The social thought of Vivekananda mainly rests on the Vedantic spiritual ideals of solidarity and divinity of man. It has pursued the practical application of these higher truths for the betterment of the society. The Vedantic conception of oneness of the divine spirit which is the base of the ideal of social morality is aptly applied for social cohesion. It establishes that the oneness of mankind is a fact and not a fable. It calls forth the spiritual unity of all living things and the totality of all existence. Thus instead of universal brotherhood the thought announces universal selfhood which precipitates to the view that every action will affect the organic unity of human life. In such a deeply integrated cosmic life-vision every action tends to produce a great impact on other beings just like a wave in the ocean. It is this deep-rooted interconnection that makes one aware of the interdependency in social life. Accordingly spiritual enlightenment of man and social activity do not stand mutually aggressive; rather a social worker becomes a better worker when he derives sustenance from spiritual experience and arms himself with spiritual power. Being in such a position his thought can aptly be placed under the group of socio-spiritualism which correlates secular with the spiritual sphere.

With his penetrative outlook, Vivekananda realizes that the remedy for individual and social distortion lies in the continuation of man's evolution, beyond the organic level into the spiritual level. He held that no amount of political reform, economic regeneration, or increase in the amenities of life can ever insure the peace and well-being of the society. On the otherhand he attaches great importance to spiritual values in understanding the social context. Hence his thought does not fall under the category of Western philosophers like Rousseau or Marx, nor can he considered as a pure spiritualist in the narrow sense of the term. For him spirituality does not mean the art of transmitting information of the after-world, but is the pursuit of the knowledge regarding the divinity and the solidarity of the soul which forms the main theme of Vedanta. He never tried to keep religion and spirituality out from the social realm as did the thinkers of his age. Vivekananda was convinced of the fact that social progress is not possible in India, unless it is based on religion.

He was of the opinion that society could be improved not by the removal of any religions rather by applying them in society as they should have to be. Though he was aware of religious fanaticism born out of narrow regional outlook, he did not want to throw away the baby with bathwater. Moreover, he opines that when a particular sect or a religion is abolished, it will cause another one to sprout. To add a new cult to the existing list is to multiply the causes of human division and thence of human strife in the society. Vivekananda's idea of universal religion affirms that it is not the birth, but man's inner likes and choices that determine his religion. So it becomes clear that, Vivekananda while trying to individualize religion, it gets universalized. In order to explain the nature of true religion, he adopted a form of syncretism, a synthetic approach that seeks the common base for different religions. However, the basic unity of religions does not call for uniformity of faith. His observation that "it is very good to be born in a church, but it is very bad to die there"[2] is actually against sectarianism. His thoughts on religion are a pointer to the fact that human beings normally adhere to forms and ceremonies throughout their lives and fail rising to spirituality, the essence of religion.

Religion has got various shades of meanings and implications in Vivekananda's thought. He was not a prophet of religion in the ordinary sense and did not believe in a religion confined in theories or sectarianism. His thought stresses that the expression of religion must change along with the social situation. It must not be a life-negating affair consisting of a blend of illogical beliefs or presumptions as in the ancient times. Instead religion must be a life transforming force. This only can redeem the society from the disunity, disharmony, divisiveness and destruction of everything that we consider to be valuable and abiding. The root meaning of the word religion itself is that which unites, unites man to man and man to God. So that which unites is religion, but today we find just the opposite. Those who accept religion and condoned crimes against humanity in the name of religion are truly irreligious and even anti-religious in Vivekananda's vision. The thought which is preferential to Vivekananda is all-inclusive an Advaitic catholicity than the usual expression of mere religious tolerance. In fact, his thought is a cursor to the fact that so long as man holds intolerable social and religious distinctions, he is not religious at all. Here there is a perceptive impact of Vivekananda's teaching on the modern society.

---

[2].*The Complete Works of Swami Vivekananda*, Vol.2, p. 39.

Vivekananda has viewed religion as a process of evolution of dynamic faith towards spiritual destiny. He considers religion as realisation, awakening the inherent divinity of soul which every man has *in potentio*. It is a question of being and becoming, not of merely believing. To find God, Vivekananda advised that man must look within and not in theories or doctrines enshrined in holy books. Religion is the idea which raises the brute to man and man to God. This shifting of God from a far off heaven to the heart of every being as his inner most self marks advancement in the spiritual history of the world. A truly religious man who feels the reality of God in his very pulse and nature can dedicate himself and work for the mankind selflessly. To be divine and to do well to others form the essence of Vivekananda's religion. Thus his idea of religion as self-discovery is not an escape from social struggle. On the other hand it is through the exercise of religion, spiritual wisdom and social affairs are brought into an intimate relationship. It is time for the progressive people of our present society to consider whether they should, instead of pinning God for the kingdom of God, strive to make human society more humane by looking upon the teaching of Vivekananda that sees man as the embodiment of god.

Vivekananda's conception of religion is not, in anyway a kind of escapism instead it stands for a life of activity and services to mankind because for him religion is realisation of the solidarity of man. It consist not mere sacerdotal elements but also contains essentials for progressing from an ego-centric life to an all-centred life. In contrast with the religion of ancient times which condemned the poor the miserable and the exploited on the belief that their condition was borne of previous karma, this new religion of Vivekananda looks upon them as veritable Gods. It unifies people of varying places and races with its inherent vision of universal selfhood. His universal religion regards mankind as one and divine and considers service to the poor and the down trodden as true worship. This is similar to Tagore's religion that pursues God not by chanting and telling of beads but by seeing and serving Him in the tiller and in the path maker. Vivekananda's fervour in respect of service to others made him write: *Vasanthavallokahitamcharantah* – Doing good to others (silently) like the spring."[3] Here, both humanism and humanitarianism are combined in his religion. He tries to give to his philosophy a humanistic garb recommending humanitarian work and service. Thus religion in Vivekananda's thinking opens the way for social reconstruction and progress.

Vivekananda traced the reason for India's downfall as the over-emphasis given on renunciation and mysticism and thereby neglecting the social feeling and action. The religion he upholds is not a life-negating affair divorced social concerns. The social insinuation in his concept of religion distinguishes him from other great thinkers of his age. He reveals the follies in talking religion and metaphysics to the poor and the needy without satisfying their basic needs. His maxim 'first bread, then religion', emphasizes the need of ensuring minimum economic security to every

---

[3]SwamiVivekananda, *The Complete Works of Swami Vivekananda* (Kolkata: Advaita Ashrama, 2005), Vol.7, pp.486-7.

human being in order to pursue his spiritual goal. The economic contend of Vivekananda's philosophy is exposed here. Thus the philosophy that he puts forward is meant for rescuing the people who were caught between the Scylla of plain materialism and the Charybdis of religious materialism.

Vivekananda has suggested what he terms 'toned down' materialism for the purpose of providing a qualitative and healthy social life for his countrymen. His thought that does not turn its face towards material advancements while accepting spirituality and spiritual development of the individual. Excessive emphasis laid upon single aspect of life may lead to the imbalance between the society and the individual being. The material values that are gained on the basis of spiritual value of righteousness will definitely direct man to an elevated life. But being stagnant at the level of organic pleasure and satisfaction will lead him to a degenerated state. The means and goals of spiritual culture as well as the material ideals are equally necessary for the proper functioning of the social order. The ultimate end of life or self-realisation is not an other-worldly affair, but that which necessitates concentration of all human energies inward in the world of spirit which makes the ground for a synthetic vision of unity and calls for the selfless service to the society. As the triple pursuits of life, *dharma, artha* and *kama* which form the social manifestations of the three basic urges of man namely thought, action and desire need not be censored as it may lead to disturbances to the individual and conflict in the society. Thus the thought demands a harmony of biological and spiritual plane of existence. The human being must be ensured of minimum economic security in order to pursue his spiritual goal of god realization undisturbed by anxiety and care.

A society which recognizes and harmonizes matter and spirit, is recommended in the social thought of Vivekananda. But he observes with regrets that such society is equally missing in the East and in the West. Envisaging material prosperity as a friend and not the foe of spiritual regeneration, Vivekananda urged upon his countrymen to be adequately sensible to the material values of life. Therefore the thought which he put forwarded for the upliftment of society, aims at creating a synthesis of materialism of the West and spiritualism of the East. Hence an integral approach with regard to the aim of life is established. Recognizing spiritualism and materialism as the two integral elements of human culture, he proclaims a synthesis of the two in the modern age, thus advocating a give and take policy for the construction of an ideal society.

Vivekananda was adaptive to values that world over have. His vision concerning the importance of exchange of intellectual and social ideas for the proper development of society is revealed when he encourages comparison of Eastern and Western ideals and promotes its synthesis. Vivekananda while trying to create a synthesis of materialism of the West and Spiritualism of the East aimed at creating a synthesis of the demands man's inner and outer life. In fact, the thought and personality of Vivekananda exhibit a reconciliation of the saintliness of the East and the manliness of the West. He appreciated certain qualities like faith in themselves and cooperative spirit which the eastern wisdom endorses. He observes the manifestation of these qualities more in the Western people. Through the power of organization, he observed, a rapid social progress could be ensured in the West. That the westerners could put aside all differences and work in a cooperative and organized manner required some degree of transcendence of the ego but helped in creating a harmonious society. Hence he exhorts Indians to acquire and imbibe the methods of organization and self-confidence from the Western people along with their scientific and technological knowledge. Advocating the immaterial and implicit dimension in Indian spiritual tradition, he wanted the West to have a spiritual base and wanted the East to assimilate what was best in the West in order to make a social progress.

The oriental ideal is a necessity for the progress of the human race as is the occidental. He noticed that the crucial cause of the downfall of India is that the nation never had the opportunity to blend with other nations. The blind negation was not a cultural approach, rather he wanted each nation to cooperate with other nations and accept and assimilate useful and adaptable ideas from them as a complete civilization requires suitable blending of ideals, both of its own and of other nations. Many of the reform movements in India, he observes have failed because of its attempt to abolish culture and customs while trying to root out the social evils. As a nation cannot sustain on its tradition alone, Vivekananda was adaptive to values that the world has all over. He says that there cannot be equality when one party is always the teacher and the other party sits always at his feet. A man or society which has nothing to learn is in the jaws of death, its destruction is inevitable. Therefore he wanted both the Eastern and Western worlds to interact freely and simultaneously with each other following the principle of give and take. While conserving one's own cultural identity one must nurture oneself with the world culture. This is the technique Vivekananda upholds for expansion and evolution of the individual and of the society.

A vision regarding the importance of exchange of intellectual and social ideas for the proper development of society is explored throughout Vivekananda's work. Both the East and West have to supply and hand down for the accomplishment of an ideal and harmonious society. He felt the necessity to compare the Eastern and Western ideas and to adopt a social system which synthesized what is best in the Western tradition and the perennial Indian thought. While weighing the strengths and weaknesses of Eastern and Western societies, he noticed yet another fact that distinguishes both the societies   regarding the matter of individualism and socialism. It was the social freedom enjoyed by the people of the West which gives opportunity to the lowest in society. But in India, on the contrary the individual needs to be fit into the system at any cost because of its emphasis on society's good than on the individual's. As freedom is the only condition for growth, any progress either it is concerned with individual or on society is dependent entirely on it. Hence the India society with all its restrictions except for renunciates could produce only a few towering personalities or spiritual giants whereas the conditions of the masses remain deplorably unprogressive in it. The exercise of the individualistic method in the western society provides ample opportunities to its masses. Actually he wanted to retain both the individualistic and socialistic ideals in his social thought. Though Vivekananda admits that there is an intimate and organic relation between the individual and the society, he asserts that the individual must be allowed to retain his freedom and dignity. In other words, individual cannot be allowed to be suppressed by the society. The society as well as the individual has got equal importance as both are interrelated as complementary poles of an integral whole. Hence there seems a synthesis of individualism and socialism in his social thought.

As a close observer of social issues Vivekananda also points out the demerits of conservatism and a blind imitation of the West. He questions the spell of imitating the West without reason, discrimination or reference to *sastras* and criticized the Indian's attitude of accepting all that the Westerners admire blindly thereby rejecting whatever things they dislike or censure. The total repudiation of the Indian customs and social ethos in toto without rational and argumentative analysis of their merits in the given social context might hamper the society. By pointing out that what is meat for a particular society or a nation may be poison for the other, he brings to light the vanity of imitating the lines of action that foreign societies have adopted. He used to remind Indians not to be pulled out of the circle of national culture while becoming captivated and seduced by the western stuff.

The social philosophy that he has developed comprises the social, moral, cultural and spiritual ideals of ancient India with the required modernity. Supporting the tradition, Vivekananda observed that the degeneration of India came not because of the laws and customs of the ancients were bad, but because they were not allowed to be carried to their legitimate conclusion. The ancient scriptures with some parts of it which were formerly half-ridden and others wholly so, have been completely revealed by Vivekananda's task of reorientation. This is justified when his thought finds consonance with the classification of society on the scheme of *Varnasrama dharma* and guided by the four *purusharthas*- Knowledge, valour, wealth and labour which form the foundation of society and whose misuse can bring disintegration in society. His thought regards diversity as the essential aspect of any society. It holds that diversity is not false by nature; however it becomes false when divorced from the Unity which is the central truth. In this relation the thought is agreeing much with a verse in the Isopanisad which has its purport that those who are devoted entirely to the principle of multiplicity and ignored the underlying Unity will exhibit their lack of knowledge; but more than that is the ignorance of those who are devoted entirely to the principle of indiscriminate Unity ignoring the multiplicity because such Unity is reduced to blank identity or void.

Since India is a spiritually oriented country, it was necessary for Vivekananda to develop a spiritual system of ideas, norms and values that would bring about a modification in the thought consciousness of the people and consequently advancement in society. Hence he is against the violent break with the Indian spiritual tradition. For him social change should be the outcome of the process of adjustment of old institutions and values to the new conditions.

In his concept of society, Vivekananda has managed to develop a kind of single community while preserving the diversity. Society is viewed as an organic union in which each component forms an integral part of the society. For this reason he does not recommend the total abolition of caste as he considers it as a natural order. But he has suggested its readjustment in accordance with the modern conditions. The organic union with its many different components and all are essentially complete while preserving the diversity. It shows that the society functions as a well co ordinate single unit; in it none is inferior to the other. All are equally important and cooperative action of all these components are essential for the proper functioning of society. Each individual member of society must fulfill a certain function in it, thus contributing to the general welfare of the social structure as a whole. Vivekananda maintains that each component forms an integral part of the society and in the absence of one, the society fails to exist and function. By fulfilling the demands of both the inner and the outer life of the individual, it aimed at social progress.

Vivekananda put his finger on the evils of modern perverted caste system that kept the downtrodden masses away from the mainstream of the society. It is true that he had no repugnance towards the caste system of our ancient society as he considered it as the natural order of any society. For him whatever nature gathers and provides us like of power, wisdom, and wealth as such is not necessarily an evil, but he realized that these are all for diffusion whenever needed. But if power, wisdom, and wealth were left concentrated in the hands of a few by ignoring the aforesaid truth, they can become a social evil. The social thought of Vivekananda points out the absolute necessity of dispersion of all knowledge, wealth and power concentrated in certain families or castes to be dispersed all over the society for its welfare. He has foreseen the destruction of the society with the suspension of this diffusion and wanted a decentralization of power. Thus he strictly objected privileges and prejudices that the caste system of modern period had brought in. The distorted caste system in the modern period is a hindrance to the progress of Indian society as it keeps the downtrodden masses away from the main stream of society. Vivekananda objected this kind of ill treatment of the people of the lower strata in the name of caste and custom. By depicting casteism and untouchability as an orthodox superstition and as a type of mental disease of the upper classes he tried to express his regret in a severe manner.

Another characteristic feature of Vivekananda's social philosophy lies in its principle of leveling up and not leveling down. The solution that he put forward regarding the social problem of class and caste differences rests not in the degradation of those who are already high up, but by uplifting those who are at a low level through quality education and imparting Vedantic knowledge. Without a spiritual base all our endeavour for the betterment of the downtrodden would be impossible. That is the grounds on which he required the Brahmins to manifest their spirituality by raising others to their status. A societal patron has to realize his spiritual nature and also the spiritual nature of the masses whom he is trying to elevate. The well being of the higher classes lies in helping the lower to get their legitimate rights. His philosophy is a philosophy of love which does not encourage class struggle. Thus the thought of spirituality that he put forwarded remains a fit medium for preservation and promotion of humanistic values.

Vivekananda perceives that it is the attitude of the work done that makes distinctions in the society. What makes a man superior is not his caste but the quality which he possesses. What Vivekananda wants to convey here is that each person is responsible for what he is. When one engages oneself with another for pay or is busy transacting some piece for profit, he pitches himself in *sudrahood* and *vaisyahood* respectively. Here he intends to convey the message that any work done without expecting anything in return elevates that person to *brahminhood*. Work done with a master's mind puts one really in a high position. Vivekananda teaches that no duty is ugly or impure and it is the circumstances that make one perform a particular job. Any work done in sincerity and detachment can make one illumined. On the basis of views of Vivekananda, the highest culture resides in the conception of ideal *Brahminhood*. In this connection he also writes that *Brahminhood* cannot be associated with exclusive privilege of a few. An essential part of Vivekananda thought, lies in the emphasis he puts on work done in a sincere and detached manner. Any work done in such a way can make one illumined. This is the reason why he avers that "birth is nothing, the environment is everything". He states that it is not the birth but dharma and virtuous conduct that makes one a *Brahmin*. Therefore he holds the possibility for one to be transformed from one caste supporting caste mobility. Here it follows that everyone is responsible for what he is. One could change his caste by acquiring the necessary qualities through the performance of *karma*. He stood against the stiff and rigid caste distinctions which were opposed to the religions of Vedanta stand as a barrier to Indian's progress. Instead, the emphasis the thought stresses on caste mobility can make everyone to an elevated state and can contribute to social progress.

Vivekananda conceived the idea of privilege as a bane to society as they form hindrance to social equality. In society, however we have come across various inequalities of various types. While analysing different kinds of privileges – privilege of strong over the weak, that of the rich over the poor, of a man who has more money than another and privilege based on more learning, he realised that the worst one and most tyrannical is the privilege of spirituality because of its claim to know more of spirituality and of God. But Vivekananda holds that those who demand any such privileges can neither be a Vedantist nor an illumined person, as he could not realise the God that exists in every human soul. Since every man is actually divine, the same power, the same consciousness lies in every one of us. It follows that all are possessors of infinite knowledge and that all knowledge is in every soul, even in the most ignorant who might not have had the opportunity to manifest his knowledge in the same manner as done by someone else, since his environment was not suitable. Thus the idea that one man is born superior to the other or one man possesses more knowledge and hence deserves a superior status, has no relevance in accordance with the philosophy of Vivekananda.

It is not possible for any social philosophy to survive by neglecting the masses of a country who act as an indispensable link and foundation for the overall growth of the nation. Vivekananda has noticed that the vast majority of people of his are suffering in poverty, squalor, disease and ignorance and a select few live in comfort, luxury, power and position. He has tried to solve these problems related to the contrast of wealth and poverty, of despotism and degradation recommending curtailment of want, exaltation of poverty and to practice charity and the development of a kind and sympathetic attitude to the lowly and exploited. As a social thinker, his endeavour is to create conditions in which inequalities cannot grow and not simply ironing out the differences. For this purpose he has based the foundation of his socialism in the Vedantic precept of spiritual equality and universal salvation. The equalizing theories put forward by him has much connection to his assertion that apart from the Whole, the existence of the individual is inconceivable as an individual's life is in the life of the Whole and the individual's happiness is entirely dependent on the happiness of the Whole. Thus the socialism that he upholds is a movement where by the individuals acted freely and spontaneously for the good of the whole society. Advocating the modern principle of equality of opportunity, Vivekananda acquires a socialistic garb. His thought finds no justification on the plea that the inequality and the consequent suffering of *sudra* was due to the *karma* in their previous life. In this context his utterances are pragmatic in tone. His effort to raise the standard of the weak and the down trodden was mainly to maintain a social egalitarianism. He tried to uphold equal status for all sections of people in the society. By pleading for their freedom and equal status, he envisaged an ideal society that would provide the resources as well as the opportunity for each of its members to develop his or her potential to the maximum.

Vivekananda realised the fact that it was the lack of formal education that pushed the weaker sections farther backward culturally and intellectually over the centuries. To say that other human beings do not need or do not deserve formal education and other amenities that the upper classes enjoy is to dehumanize them. In order to bring equality in society, he suggested the need of providing the poor and the weak in the society with additional opportunities for the development of their innate faculties. Vivekananda urged that the attention of the educated men to work for the emancipation of the poor instead of ignoring them. He observed that the upper classes have trodden them down by denying education which in turn made them forget their human identity. A nation is advanced in proportion only as education and intelligence spread among the masses. Opposing the tendency of monopolizing education in the hands of a few, he pleaded for the education of millions of the rural masses. Thus he envisaged the modern idea about social education. Vivekananda noticed that starting new schools was not enough for poor boys to acquire education since most of them were forced to join and help their parents in making a living. Realising the impracticality regarding such venture he suggested that the poor boy cannot approach an educational institution, the education must reach them at the plough, in the factory and everywhere. This goal could only be achieved he suggested, with the assistance of single minded, self-sacrificing *sannyasins*. These *sannyasins* could be organized to travel from village to village for teaching the common people. Here his position differed from that of Plato, who made no provision for the education of the lowest classes, but only concentrated on the development of individuality of the ruling class. But it seems to him that in modern period the West has achieved much prosperity because of the penetration of education and civilization amongst its masses. Hence he urged the necessity of spreading education along with culture to the weaker sections of people who were pushed culturally and intellectually for the overall development of society.

Culture, which comprises one of the principal components of preparation of life in society, plays a meticulous role in its development. Each nation and each separate civilization finds development in its own culture that had its roots in generations hundreds and thousands of years ago. In the case of individuals what comprise his culture is his inner growth, the way he behaves to others and his capacity to understand the other person. Vivekananda holds that through Sanskrit language, the great classics of India or the above mentioned fundamental basic truths could be fully grasped with all its relevance. Being the treasure house of ancient wisdom the study of the Classics can lead to cultural upheaval amongst the downtrodden masses who are placed in a very low esteem in the society. Because of this reason, he suggests broadening the access of Sanskrit education to all sections of the society. He had foreseen the possibility of less distinctions and more capacity to work together if the society is based on such great wisdom that the great classics had in store. It has much relevance even in the present day society as culture accelerates man's capacity to work together, making them creative, innovative, open to change capable of building permanent social bonds preventing exclusion and social pathologies thereby promotes social integration.

Vivekananda's concern for women was intense as they form the core of every family which is a miniature of society. They have undeniable influence over other members of the family. Supporting the Manu's saying that 'where women are happy, there will be prosperity,' he has given them a high esteem in the society. Vivekananda considers man and women as the two wheels of the society, without the effective working of the two, the society cannot progress. He never accepted inequality between the sexes as the Vedanta claims that the same conscious self is present in all beings .He was quite aware of the degenerated state of women of his time and vehemently criticized evils like child marriage, polygamy, sati, denial of education to girls and other evils imposed on womenfolk.

Vivekananda framed a very clear and distinct idea regarding the institution of marriage and the duties of a house holder. He considers marriage as a social institution rather than a matter of individual concern as in India more importance is given to society than individual choices. He is in perfect agreement with the Indian conception of marriage which is meant to perpetuate race and not for sense gratification. A householder shall have a life established in Supreme Reality and dedicate his life to him by which individual instincts are subordinated. Again he warned that if individual pleasures or satisfaction of animal instincts were the criterion in selecting one's life partner, the result must be brutal children who will be responsible for the evil of society. Hence he says that so long as one lives in society, he must sacrifice his personal desire for public good. In realizing the ideal society envisioned by Vivekananda both the monk and the house holder have to make their contribution.

As a progressive thinker he was against the irrationality of forbidding inter-caste marriages. He held that in the absence of inter caste marriage; the race will become much weaker. So he was against the tendency of keeping marriage relations confined within the limited socio cultural unit of a single society. He censured the marriage alliance between cousins and near relatives even at a time when they were quite prevalent. With far sightedness he opined that such marriage will deteriorate the race. Hence he wanted to widen the circle of marriage in order to save the progeny from diseases and other consequent evils. Regarding inter provincial marriages he prophesied that it may take a long time to attain such a progress in society. He was not in haste and adopted a way of moderation in the process of social change.

As a man of enculturation Vivekananda's vision regarding women is a unique synthesis of the East and the West and of the past and the present. By comparing the state of women in India with that of the West he realized their pathetic condition in his own country. He wanted Indian women to acquire the qualities of self-reliance and independence which he noticed among the women of the West. He also had a great admiration for the men in the West whom he conceived as the real 'sakti-worshippers'. Witnessing the freedom that the Western women enjoyed made him raise the voice against the poor conditions which the women of his country were held. In order to raise Indian women from their states of utter helplessness and servile dependency he yearned for providing them with good education, freedom, rights and equal status which the women in the West have enjoyed. He warns that any attempt on the part of the Indian women to jump out of their old spiritual inheritance will lead her to degeneration. He felt that both the cultures have their own merits and demerits and cannot judge one with the standard of the other. His thought carves out an ideal woman, as a combination of the eastern ideal of womanhood centering round motherhood, and the self-dependency and other active virtues which the western women imbibe, for the progress of society.

It is high time that our educators gave pervious thought to the education of women as women. It must be an effective one to take them to a position where they themselves can solve their problem. For this purpose the scheme of female education propounded by Vivekananda would serve as an ideal one. It is meant for the self-sufficiency and for their better participation in the society. Although men and women are equally competent for academic work, women have a special aptitude for and competence in studies related to home and family. It might be perhaps on knowing this fact, Vivekananda justly suggested them to imbibe lessons of housekeeping, duties of home life and principles that helps them form an ideal character, and thereby they will be fit enough for taking the big responsibility of being a mother to perfection. He envisioned that only in the homes of an educated and pious mother that the great men will be born. He also stressed the need for good parentage. It is the prenatal influence that gives the impetus to the child for good and evil. Hence Vivekananda realised that there is nothing greater for social improvement than bringing up a healthy, intelligent and cultured generation which only an educated and pious mother can provide.

The necessary regrounding of society, for Vivekananda would have to be facilitated through authentic education. Without authentic knowledge concerning individual and of society as a whole, there was no chance for real development that brings about the best in a given society. It can purge our minds of age-old prejudices and set our faces against the trivialities of life. Anyway Vivekananda was not satisfied with the educational system of his time. He criticized the attitude in our education system which centers more on details concerning things outside our own nation and paying least importance for own tradition and culture. By emphasizing the need for learning the wisdom of Indian tradition along with Western Sciences and knowledge, he demanded a thorough change in the existing education system.

The end and aim of all training according to him is to make man grow not only intellectually but mentally and spiritually. Man is a harmonious blend of body, mind and spirit just as Descartes thinks of man as an organic whole. He disliked knowledge and skills-driven educational approach devoid of emphasis on spiritual evolution of man. By comparing spiritual training with 'rice' and every other sources of knowledge with curries, he says in a simple manner that taking curries alone cause indigestion and so is the case with taking rice only, stressed the need of both secular and spiritual education. Hence he professed incorporating all that is best in the occidental education system to that of the East. Thus trans-culturally oriented Vivekananda had the hope that India would set an example of how science and religion could meet, science taking care of man's physical needs and religion, of his moral and spiritual needs. It is not that type of education that puts information into the brain of the student that he recommended. But for him the education should ennoble the individual to develop himself into a balanced personality, a total man, fit to discharge his social obligations.

The personal influence of the teacher in imparting education is very great indeed. And that is the reason why Vivekananda suggests the adoption of ancient residential institutions of education where students and teachers can live together and have an exchange of ideas. A comprehensive and fruitful preparation for life as a whole can be achieved by the careful attention of the teacher who is a man of character. Thus he pleaded for a man-making, life-giving, character-building education by which a complete living is made possible through the harmony of physical, mental, intellectual and spiritual training. A country's future depends on the attitude of its people. Hence he recommends that type of education which enables him to enhance his nature making him free from suspicion, jealousy and conceit and thereby make him lead a cooperative and mutually helpful life. Here his educational view stands close to that of Bertrand Russell's who states its aim as developing minds sensitive enough to perceive and feel the shocks of tragedies taking place in societies.

The scheme of education Vivekananda suggests is meant for the expansion of heart and not mere intellectualism. Education is a process of manifestation of perfection already in man. The end and aim he conceived of education is to make man grow towards perfection. Recognizing mental slums as more dangerous than material slums, he states that there is no need of polishing up the outside without refining his inner side. It reveals the truth that learning or attaining education without being truly cultured, a man becomes a danger and threat to society. There is an observation of Aristotle which is akin to this saying: "Man when perfected is the best of animals, but when separated from law and justice, he is the worst of all, since armed injustice is most dangerous".[4] In the same way Vivekananda also states that education without morality is worse than having no education at all.

In giving the shape to the ideal society envisaged by Vivekananda, the contribution of the youth cannot be overestimated. Youth of any nation sketches the cause of drastic social and political changes. They should achieve strength physically, mentally and spiritually, so that they can approach life's problems with the fortitude, self-control and a sense of balance. The social conditions of past, present and future or of any places demand such a youth with character and democratic discipline. Vivekananda's inspiring messages even now as in the past make the youth awake with a sense of exhilaration and the buoyancy of spirit for the cause of social reconstruction. When it comes to building up a modern Indian society, it was upon the youth that he puts greater faith upon. He felt that as the youth had no possession, they could be the sincere and dedicated souls. Because they are sincere, they can give up

---

[4]Paul Mackendrick and Herbert.M.House, ed., *Classical in translation* (England: The University Wisconsin Press, 1952), Vol.1, p.353.

their all for a noble cause of nation-building. That is why Vivekananda reposed full confidence on the youth to participate in the venture of eradicating all evils of the Indian society and for achieving freedom of all kind, political, social and spiritual. He wanted the youth to understand their immense inner potentialities and energy and to use them in bringing back Indian's ancient glory.

Vivekananda holds that the inactivity and a sense of helpless dependence of young people can bring down restraints to social progress. He tried to infuse the Vedantic ideals like understanding one's own divinity, karma yoga, *thyaga* (sacrifice), *sraddha* (faith in oneself) and *abhaya* (fearlessness) etc. into the minds of the youth. He wanted to bring back their lost manliness by cultivating the faith in oneself. What he meant is to wake up from delusion and laziness, work for overcoming the social backwardness and ignorance by developing intellectual strength and power of will. Spiritual knowledge of one's own self, one becomes self-confident. Believing in one's own self is the beginning of all virtues.

Strength, both physical and mental was yet another theme on which Vivekananda harped incessantly for youth in order to make them capable to contribute for the social welfare. He wanted to apply the teaching of the Upanisadic dictum, *Nayamatma balahinena labhya* which means that the self cannot be realized by the weak to the individual as well as the collective life. Practice of spirituality dissociated from worldly context is bogus. Body is regarded as the instrument for righteous living. He was of the opinion that only a physically strong individual can have complete control over his body as well as mind. With this end in view he laid great stress on physical culture. A sound mind necessarily presupposes a sound body. The necessity of acquiring a strong healthy physique for the attainment of moral and spiritual strength is emphasized through passage like "Atman cannot be attained by those who are physically and mentally weak." And again "You will be nearer to heaven through football than through the study of the Gita" also convey the same intend. Here also one can find an approach which lays emphasis on physical as well as mental strength thereby giving the scope of harmony in his thought. Through inspiring speeches, he urged the youth to build up a modern vibrant society free from poverty and disease, rational and non-superstitious, where there is communal harmony, mutual respect, where women are respected and there is all round cooperation in bringing about development.

Vivekananda's thought of preserving the tradition while adopting foreign ideas has much significance and relevance in the present societal contexts, especially in the milieu of the decline in many walks of modern life. In modern India, the two maxims of Indian culture, morality and spirituality seem to be diminishing in its import. The modern India is in front of an acute crisis of preserving its distinctiveness in culture and spirituality with westernization and globalization, bringing about negative impacts in the life style of its people. The population of India is in need of the acceptance of a relevant practical social philosophy in order to lead their personal as well as social life in tune with the culture and heritage of the country. It is high time that the current situation in India is to be remoulded on the basis of the teachings of Vivekananda which are good guidelines in the construction of a better society. It is the unique feature of his social thought to comprehend the unity underlying the apparent diversity by seeking continuity of the present with the past in which it is rooted and its projection into the future. Vivekananda wants to keep a balance between stability and change, tradition and modernity. That is why his thought maintains a 'move on' rather than 'reform'. He wanted changes to happen in a society by evolution, by preserving tradition, rather than by revolution.

As stated before Vivekananda was also a person of enculturation and had extensive knowledge on Indian as well as on thoughts across the world. Hence his thought remains the foremost one which confronted the questions of caste, religion, minority issue, modernism, economics and social issues of India and it brought a refreshing view point to the same. His teachings are meant to alleviate both the spiritual as well as material poverty of man. Along with its emphasis on spiritual nature, his thought does not degrade or despise the human body. Hunger, mal nutrition and disease which are due to poverty are symptoms of material illness of a society in which there is exploitation of one group by another. There is therefore the need of rendering help to the poor through proper reorganization of the structure of the society. The disregard of the body of a person because of birth or caste, or gender is a symptom of social illness arising from the concept of discrimination operating in society. This again calls for a rearrangement of social relations among the people with an effective social philosophy. Vivekananda's social philosophy is a comprehensive one which encompasses past and present, tradition and modernity, theory and practice and one which combines in itself the spiritual and secular thoughts of the East and the

West. The thought correlates individualism with socialism, materialism and spiritualism, absolutism and pantheism, the One and the many for the proper social development. His thought is also an attempt that aims at an integral development of the human person in the context of society.

Harmony, concord and Unity forms the essential principles of his thought. To Vivekananda, 'No progress without contradiction for any civilization,' as asserted by Karl Marx is just an arbitrary statement. If disharmony, discord and distrust form the base of any society it may censor its growth possibility. It is Unity and not disunity that is the inherent order of the cosmos and whatever runs in contrast to this would be unsustainable, he believed. His thought aims to develop unity out of diversities and coherence out of incoherence. In fact this forms the essence of the teachings of Advaita, the real monism which helps humanity to know its inner informing spirit. This is what Vivekananda believed as the very purpose of life.

According to Vivekananda the progress of the world depends upon social evolution, social progress upon individual development and individual expansion upon the spiritual awakening of man. He has the firm conviction that unless man spiritualises his life and discovers his potential divinity, he cannot effectively solve any problem related to peace and harmony in the world. Hence he wanted the worldly purpose to be informed by a high spirituality. In his perception human life and in fact the entire universe is an indivisible totality. Vivekananda revived the spiritual vision as an intimate vision, a pervasive feeling in which one sees all as oneself feels all as oneself and serves all as one self. Spiritual awakening is a matter of living a